Really Easy Play with Trumps

The English Bridge Union

Published by the English Bridge Union in England 2012

© English Bridge Union Ltd 2012

ISBN 0-9506279-8-4

Typeset by Wakewing of High Wycombe
Printed and bound by Charlesworth Press, Wakefield

The Radio Society of Great Britain
3 Abbey Court
Fraser Road
Priory Business Park
Bedford
MK44 3WH

really easy play with trumps

Really Easy Play with Trumps is for all those less experienced bridge players who want to gain a firm grasp of the basics and improve their card play in suit contracts.

The book spends time introducing the basics thoroughly, thus giving the sound grounding that is essential to develop as a successful declarer. Whilst not covering all the more complex plays in suit contracts, the most common techniques are introduced and discussed. In just one or two places, you might feel the book moves beyond the Really Easy stage to give you a glimpse of the reason why you never get tired of playing the game.

All bidding sequences given are in Standard English, all defensive leads and signals are made to the Standard English agreements. This method, based on Acol and the weak no trump opening, is the English Bridge Union's recommended starting point for those learning the game.

Study this book and your play will improve by leaps and bounds.

John Pain
EBUTA Manager

RULE OF 57
NO. OF TOP TRICKS?
SUBTRACT FROM 7
L - ODD
H - EVEN

S = STRENGTH
W = WEAKNESS
O = OPPORTUNITIES
T =

Other books in the Really Easy Bridge series brought to you by
Bridge for All.

Really Easy Bidding	2009
Really Easy Play in No trumps	2002
Really Easy Mistakes	2005
Really Easy Modern Acol	2007
Really Easy Defence	2009
Really Easy Competitive Bidding	2003
Really Easy Slams	2004
Practice Beginning Bridge	2005
Practice Continuing Bridge	2007

The English Bridge Union
Broadfields
Bicester Road
Aylesbury HP19 8AZ
Tel: 01296 317217
Email: bfa@ebu.co.uk

contents

the really easy bridge series

what is the aim of the series?

The Really Easy Bridge Series presents the fundamentals of the game in a clear usable way. The readers will be able to put the ideas into practice in their very next game. It is not for the expert or those who enjoy learned discussions on theory.

who is it for?

- People who can recognise a pack of cards and want to enjoy playing with them.
- Students in bridge classes who want to supplement the teaching notes.
- Those wishing to discover how to improve their card play.

how to use the book

- Always have a pack of cards by you as you read – lay out the hands to follow the play more clearly.
- Bridge is a partnership game – read this book with your partner and enjoy learning together.
- Play bridge – practice makes perfect.

This is the seventh book in the series. Further titles are on the way. Write to me at the English Bridge Union if you want your name on our mailing list.

John Pain
Bridge for All Manager

1 introduction

This book should be regarded as complementary to both *Really Easy Bidding* and *Really Easy Play in No Trumps.* The book is directed at less experienced players and aims to keep things simple so that they can be understood.

There are no explanations of the bidding. Auctions, where it is necessary to give them, are in simple Standard English.

There are some basic play techniques, which apply whether or not there is a trump suit, and it is assumed that these are understood. The techniques include opening lead conventions, cashing winners, making small cards into winners, the hold up and the finesse. Whilst not giving thorough coverage, this book does give reminders about many of these techniques.

There is no magic formula for playing the cards in the right way. One learns the basic techniques, but when you are playing a hand, you have to decide which one applies in each case. Thinking and planning are important and with practice you will get much better. But even the best players get caught out occasionally, when trumps break badly or an opponent gets an unexpected ruff; so the book does cover ways to handle some of the pitfalls too.

You will find that many of the examples are about high-level contracts – games or slams. The reason for this is to simplify the explanation of the basic principles and the logical thinking needed. In part score contracts there are 'ifs' and 'buts' and 'maybes' which confuse things but the hope is that, by understanding the basics, you will be better equipped to play those part score contracts as well.

So . . . welcome to the West seat at the table from where you will be expected to do all the work! Making up the hands with a pack of cards lets you go through the deal trick by trick. This is the best way to understand the point being made.

The book ends with thirty practice hands. The first fifteen hands are intended to be easier than the next fifteen. You can make them up and play them with friends but do make sure everyone has a turn at being West.

Two bridge terms, extensively used, merit a definition:

- Drawing trumps means to play cards in the trump suit until the defenders' trumps have all been removed.

- 'To ruff' or 'ruffing' means exactly the same as 'to trump' or 'trumping' – that is to play a trump to a trick when unable to follow suit.

Remember to have a pack of cards ready as you read the book.

2 trumps v no trumps

A no trump contract is simple: during the play, the highest card of the suit led wins the trick. Even the lowest card, the two, is a winner if it is led and none of the other players is able to follow suit.

A contract which specifies a trump suit (called a 'suit' contract) means that, provided a player has no cards left in the suit being played, he has the option of using a trump to win the trick. An ace, sure to win a trick in a no trump contract, can lose to a two in the trump suit.

So, when would you prefer a suit contract rather than no trumps? Put very simply, your decision should depend on two factors:

■ Can you WIN more tricks in a suit contract than in a no trump contract?

■ Could you LOSE more tricks by choosing either alternative?

Here is an example:

```
            ♠ A K 10 9           N            ♠ Q J 8 7
            ♥ 7 4 3        W           E      ♥ 9 8 6
            ♦ A K Q                           ♦ 9 7 5
            ♣ A J 4              S            ♣ K Q 2
```

Suppose, as West, you could see your partner's hand before you decided what the final contract should be. You count your top winners, which comes to ten – one more than you need to make 3NT.

However, you must look at the number of tricks that you could lose. You will lose none in three of the suits, but how many would you lose in hearts if North were to lead them?

In theory, it could be as many as seven if North had all the outstanding hearts! That is very unlikely, of course, but there is certainly a risk that that the defence may take five heart winners immediately.

In a no trump contract, it is no use having nine or more winners if the defenders take five tricks before you gain the lead.

With the hands given, you would certainly want to play in a game contract but, because you might lose too many heart tricks at the start, you would reject 3NT and choose game in a suit contract. 4♠ is the obvious choice because:

■ Spades is the longest combined suit (West + East).

■ You can count the required ten top winners.

■ You avoid losing more than three heart tricks because you can trump the fourth round of the suit. If you trump in one hand there are still four top trump winners in the other hand.

Suppose North cashed three top heart winners, ♥A K Q and then played another heart. You would trump this in either the East or West hand and discard a club or a diamond from the other hand.

As well as this trick, you have nine more winners.

The complete deal might be

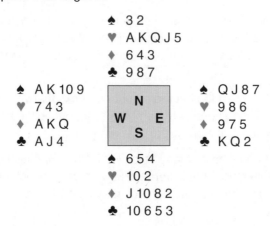

In this deal the trumps are very strong. East/West actually have the eight top trumps. But most of the time the trumps will be weaker. Suppose the spades are

♠ A K Q 2   ▭   ♠ 6 5 4 3

Is it still correct to choose to play in spades? After all, we are missing ♠J 10 9 8 7. Remember these five missing spades are distributed between the North and South hands. This might be

In fact, this distribution of three in one hand and two in the other happens about 68% of the time. This suit can never make more than four tricks in no trumps but, in a spade contract, has the potential to make five tricks. Playing ♠A K Q draws the opponents' trumps and, if either ♠6 or ♠2 can be used to ruff in another suit, the combination makes five tricks.

You would be really unlucky to find

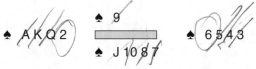

A break where one hand has four trumps is pretty unlikely – about 28% of the time, but even here you have the potential to make up to five trump tricks. Playing ♠A K Q reveals the bad break, but you might be able to ruff a loser in another suit with either ♠6 or ♠2 to bring the tally to four tricks. If you are very lucky you might be able to ruff a loser in each hand making five tricks. In no trumps you could never make more than three tricks.

The worst of all breaks, where one defender has all five trumps, happens only about 4% of the time. It is possible, therefore, that you have made the wrong decision. Suppose that you knew not just your partner's hand but your opponents' hands as well. Your second sight might reveal:

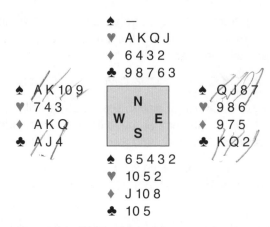

```
            ♠ —
            ♥ A K Q J
            ♦ 6 4 3 2
            ♣ 9 8 7 6 3
  ♠ A K 10 9                    ♠ Q J 8 7
  ♥ 7 4 3      ┌─────────┐      ♥ 9 8 6
  ♦ A K Q      │    N    │      ♦ 9 7 5
  ♣ A J 4      │ W     E │      ♣ K Q 2
               │    S    │
               └─────────┘
            ♠ 6 5 4 3 2
            ♥ 10 5 2
            ♦ J 10 8
            ♣ 10 5
```

With this distribution, you would be able to make nine tricks in
3NT and just the same number (one too few) in 4♠. The reason is
that the opponents' trump holding has divided 5-0. This means
that the third top winner in clubs would not make a trick since
South would trump it. Unlucky? Yes, of course, but bridge players
are always quick to tell you how unlucky they are with their bad
breaks.

Playing in a suit contract not only protects you against losing too
many tricks but can also be a means of making extra tricks.

counting trumps

There is nothing more annoying than miscounting the number of
trumps that have been played. You think that you have drawn all
the trumps but a defender unexpectedly ruffs your winner.

The best way to count trumps is the one that you can manage
(and that includes using your fingers!). Many find the easiest way
is to add together the number of trumps held between declarer
and dummy. Take this number from 13 to give the number of
trumps held by the two defenders. Whenever both defenders
follow suit, you deduct two from that total. If one defender fails to
follow suit, you deduct one.

3 the beauty of trumps

drawing trumps

Before getting too carried away with the beauty of trumps, let's step back to the basics and look at the first thing you do on most deals – drawing trumps. The following deals are essentially the same, only the trump suit changes.

You are in 4♠ on the lead of ♣Q. The ♣K loses to ♣A and South plays ♣2, which you ruff. You must lose two hearts and a club. How do you proceed?

```
                 ♠ K Q J 10 8    ┌─────────┐    ♠ A 9 6 3
                 ♥ 9 6 2         │ N       │    ♥ A 8 3
                 ♦ A K Q J       │ W     E │    ♦ 7 6 4 2
                 ♣ 3             │    S    │    ♣ K 2
                                 └─────────┘
```

Even if trumps break 4-0, draw four rounds, then cash five red suit winners for ten tricks.

```
                 ♠ Q J 10 8 7    ┌─────────┐    ♠ A 9 6 3
                 ♥ 9 6 2         │ N       │    ♥ A 8 3
                 ♦ A K Q J       │ W     E │    ♦ 7 6 4 2
                 ♣ 3             │    S    │    ♣ K 2
                                 └─────────┘
```

You cannot afford a trump loser. Lead ♠Q and play low in dummy if North plays low. Repeat the finesse if the ♠Q wins. Go down if the finesse loses, which it will half the time.

```
                 ♠ K J 8 7 5     ┌─────────┐    ♠ A 9 6 3
                 ♥ 9 6 2         │ N       │    ♥ A 8 3
                 ♦ A K Q J       │ W     E │    ♦ 7 6 4 2
                 ♣ 3             │    S    │    ♣ K 2
                                 └─────────┘
```

With nine trumps, the best play is to cash the ♠A and the ♠K, hoping that the ♠Q is either singleton or doubleton. They will be more than half the time, so playing for the queen to drop is better than taking the finesse.

```
    ♠ K J 10 8 7              ♠ A 9 6
    ♥ 9 6 2         ┌─────┐   ♥ A 8 5 3
    ♦ A K Q J       │  N  │   ♦ 7 6 4 2
    ♣ 3           W │     │ E ♣ K 2
                    │  S  │
                    └─────┘
```

With eight trumps, the queen will drop less than half the time, if you play ♠A K. Cash the ♠A and play ♠9, letting it run if South plays low.

Eight ever, nine never is the way to remember when to finesse (other things being equal).

```
    ♠ J 10 8 7 5             ♠ A 9 6 3
    ♥ K 6 2         ┌─────┐   ♥ A 8 3
    ♦ A K Q J       │  N  │   ♦ 7 6 4 2
    ♣ 3           W │     │ E ♣ K 2
                    │  S  │
                    └─────┘
```

Here you have ♥K, so can afford one trump loser. Lead the ♠J and play low from dummy if North plays low. Assuming the ♠J loses to the ♠K or ♠Q, win the return in your hand and play ♠10. Again play low from dummy if North plays low. This play only loses when South has both the ♠K and ♠Q, a quarter of the time.

trumping defenders' winners

Many declarers are happier to be playing in a suit contract than in no trumps. Perhaps the most comforting attraction is the ability to 'spike the enemy's guns'. There was an example in the previous chapter and here is another:

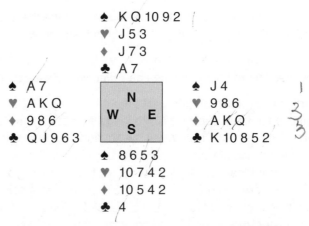

♠ K Q 10 9 2
♥ J 5 3
♦ J 7 3
♣ A 7

♠ A 7
♥ A K Q
♦ 9 8 6
♣ Q J 9 6 3

♠ J 4
♥ 9 8 6
♦ A K Q
♣ K 10 8 5 2

♠ 8 6 5 3
♥ 10 7 4 2
♦ 10 5 4 2
♣ 4

If you played in 3NT you would regret it. North would lead ♠K and, if that held, would continue with ♠Q. There are only seven top winners and you must lose the lead in order to set up the club tricks. North, of course, would win ♣A and cash three more spade tricks. One down.

You would be much happier to be in 5♣ despite the need to make eleven tricks rather than nine. You would lose ♣A, of course, but only one spade trick. Contract made.

trumping losers

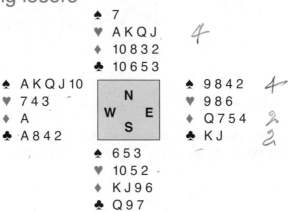

♠ 7
♥ A K Q J
♦ 10 8 3 2
♣ 10 6 5 3

♠ A K Q J 10
♥ 7 4 3
♦ A
♣ A 8 4 2

♠ 9 8 4 2
♥ 9 8 6
♦ Q 7 5 4
♣ K J

♠ 6 5 3
♥ 10 5 2
♦ K J 9 6
♣ Q 9 7

In 3NT, North has only four heart winners to take but you have a club to lose as well. With only eight top winners, the only hope for the ninth is that North holds ♣Q. You would take the finesse by leading ♣2 and playing East's ♣J but the finesse would lose.

In 4♠, you will lose the first three tricks but should not lose a club because two of your clubs can be ruffed with East's trumps.

North will switch to another suit after cashing ♥A K Q. It does matter which, but suppose North leads ♣3 at trick four. East's ♣J can be played but it is covered by ♣Q and your ♣A wins. Now just two rounds of trumps should be drawn. This leaves East's ♠9 8 to ruff those losing clubs. East's ♣K is cashed, your hand can be entered with ♦A to ruff a club and entered a second time by ruffing a diamond to trump the last club. You are left with just two master trumps.

Note that you have gained two extra tricks by ruffing in East's hand.

avoiding a loser

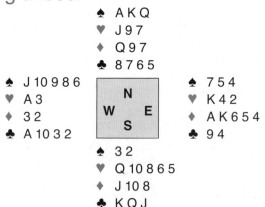

```
                    ♠ A K Q
                    ♥ J 9 7
                    ♦ Q 9 7
                    ♣ 8 7 6 5
   ♠ J 10 9 8 6          N          ♠ 7 5 4
   ♥ A 3                            ♥ K 4 2
   ♦ 3 2          W         E       ♦ A K 6 5 4
   ♣ A 10 3 2          S           ♣ 9 4
                    ♠ 3 2
                    ♥ Q 10 8 6 5
                    ♦ J 10 8
                    ♣ K Q J
```

Contract 3♠ by West. North leads ♠A K Q (South discards ♥5) and continues with ♣7 to South's ♣J and West's ♣A.

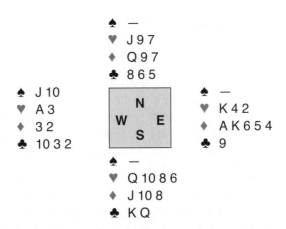

♠ —
♥ J 9 7
♦ Q 9 7
♣ 8 6 5

♠ J 10
♥ A 3
♦ 3 2
♣ 10 3 2

♠ —
♥ K 4 2
♦ A K 6 5 4
♣ 9

♠ —
♥ Q 10 8 6
♦ J 10 8
♣ K Q

Three tricks have been lost and the defence has two clubs to cash if they get in. The only suit where extra tricks can be made is diamonds which you hope break 3-3. You don't have to concede a diamond to establish the suit. Play the ♦A K and ruff ♦4. This establishes ♦6 5 as winners with ♥K as an entry to dummy to cash them. Two clubs can be discarded from your hand and the contract makes, losing just three spades and one club.

making extra tricks

A trump suit also gives much more room for manoeuvre with the opportunity of making tricks that would not be available in a no trump contract. Here are some examples:

♠ A K 7 6 5 2
♥ A 4
♦ A K 4
♣ A 3

♠ J 3
♥ 9 8 6
♦ 9 7
♣ 9 8 7 6 5 4

Any game contract is ambitious. 3NT is likely to fail on a heart lead but ten tricks in 4♠ has a better chance. You can count on making five spade tricks, assuming the probable 3-2 break, together with four top winners in the other suits. The extra trick can be made by playing ♦A K and ruffing the ♦4 in East's hand.

Extra tricks not in the trump suit (a 'side' suit) can be made by ruffing too:

♠ A K Q J 10 9	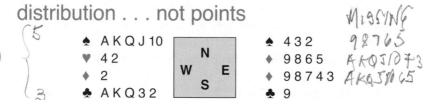	♠ 8 7 6
♥ K 7		♥ A 8 6 5 3
♦ A 2		♦ 9 8
♣ Q 4 3		♣ A K 2

In 7♠, you have only twelve top winners but need to make all thirteen. The heart suit has only two obvious winners but it has the potential to provide that vital thirteenth trick. If it divides no worse that 4-2, you will be able to establish the vital extra trick by using your own trumps.

You will win the opening lead is in your hand, draw trumps and then cash ♥K and ♥A and ruff a heart. You can then cross to dummy with a club and, if necessary, ruff another heart. If the suit splits 3-3 or 4-2, a heart winner has been established and there is still a top club in dummy as an entry to enjoy it.

distribution . . . not points

♠ A K Q J 10		♠ 4 3 2
♥ 4 2		♦ 9 8 6 5
♦ 2		♦ 9 8 7 4 3
♣ A K Q 3 2		♣ 9

In this final example you are in 4♠ on ♠5 lead. There are only eight top tricks but one more can be made by ruffing a small club in dummy. Provided clubs break 4-3, ruffing a club sets up the fifth club as a further winner.

You cash ♣A at trick two and then ruff ♣2 with one of East's trumps. The odds are that, after you win all your trump tricks and plays off ♣K Q, the lowly ♣3 will provide your tenth trick.

When the opponents hold seven of the thirteen cards in a suit it is likely that they will divide 4-3 (a 62% chance). Therefore the contract is probable rather than certain but you want to be in it despite the fact that North/South have more points (21) than East/West (19).

The beauty of trumps!

4 count winners – draw trumps?

Whatever the contract, declarer should spend time making a plan before playing a card from dummy to the first trick. It will pay a handsome dividend over the years.

It may be that you can see no way to make the contract. Maybe you should play to minimise your loss? Maybe it needs the defence to make mistakes? You don't want to throw away a certain contract with an avoidable error.

As with any no trump contract, simply take your top winners when they add up to enough tricks.

top tricks

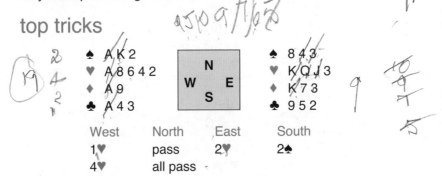

♠ A K 2		N	♠ 8 4 3
♥ A 8 6 4 2	W	E	♥ K Q J 3
♦ A 9		S	♦ K 7 3
♣ A 4 3			♣ 9 5 2

West	North	East	South
1♥	pass	2♥	2♠
4♥	all pass		

Contract 4♥ by West. North leads ♠5.

Happily, there are ten top tricks and, in a no trump contract, you could cash them in whatever order took your fancy.

Is the same true in 4♥? For sure . . . but not with the same abandon! After winning the first trick you must <u>immediately</u> play hearts in order to remove all the trumps that the defenders hold. Trying to cash a second top spade at trick two would almost certainly be fatal since a defender is allowed to ruff, just like you are.

Consider the bidding and North's lead. South probably has six spades to enter the auction as he did. This can be confirmed by North's lead. With two spades, North would lead the higher one but, here, all three cards lower than ♠5 are visible. The lead must be a singleton.

Okay . . . undue space has been taken up by stating the obvious but there is a purpose. Very often, as here, it is correct to draw trumps as soon as you can, since you must avoid a defender trumping a winner that you need. As you will see later, this is not always the case.

Meanwhile, here are some other examples when it is still right to make drawing trumps a priority.

draw trumps in the correct order

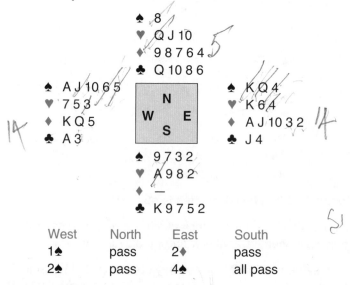

West	North	East	South
1♠	pass	2♦	pass
2♠	pass	4♠	all pass

Contract 4♠ by West. North leads ♥Q.

You should play low on the ♥Q lead since it is very unlikely North has the ♥A. It matters not what you play since defenders can always cash three rounds of hearts before switching to a club, which you win with the ♣A.

Five spades, five diamonds and one club gives eleven winners providing you play them in the correct order. Draw trumps by playing small to the ♠K first. Then ♠Q and return to your hand with ♠A. That way you can draw up to five rounds of trumps. If you play ♠A first and the spades break 4-1 you risk a diamond ruff as you try to get back to your hand to draw the last trump.

top tricks plus tricks that can be established

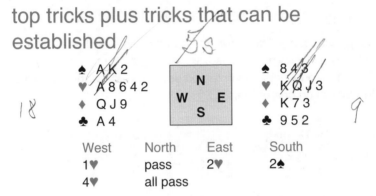

	♠ A K 2			♠ 8 4 3
	♥ A 8 6 4 2	N		♥ K Q J 3
	♦ Q J 9	W E		♦ K 7 3
	♣ A 4	S		♣ 9 5 2

West	North	East	South
1♥	pass	2♥	2♠
4♥	all pass		

Contract 4♥ by West. North leads ♠5.

Although you can count only eight top tricks, the extra two can be established by driving out ♦A. Once again, after winning the first trick, it is vital to draw trumps before playing on diamonds. In no trumps, it would be safe to establish two diamond winners immediately.

top tricks plus an extra trick by ruffing

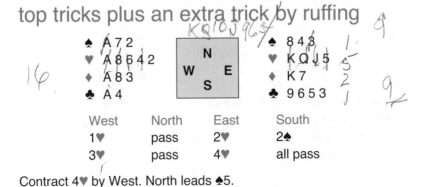

	♠ A 7 2			♠ 8 4 3
	♥ A 8 6 4 2	N		♥ K Q J 5
	♦ A 8 3	W E		♦ K 7
	♣ A 4	S		♣ 9 6 5 3

West	North	East	South
1♥	pass	2♥	2♠
3♥	pass	4♥	all pass

Contract 4♥ by West. North leads ♠5.

You count your top winners but there are only nine. However, you can see that ruffing a diamond with one of East's trumps can make the tenth trick. Draw trumps first by leading small to ♥K. If trumps are 3-1 you will have a spare trump to ruff a diamond. If trumps are 4-0 you will need to ruff a diamond before all the trumps are drawn.

lacking top winners in the trump suit

In the previous examples, drawing trumps was easy because you could play off top winners. It is still right to play trumps when you can count enough winners in the other suits – you want to avoid a defender ruffing one of them.

♠ K Q J 4 2		♠ 10 7 5 3
♥ A J 8 3	N	♥ K Q 7 2
♦ A 2	W E	♦ J 8
♣ 7 4	S	♣ A 8 3

Contract 4♠ by West. North leads ♣K.

Only six top winners can be counted but trumps will provide the other four. However, you cannot afford to allow one of your top winners to disappear because a defender ruffs it. Play a top trump and lose to ♠A . You can then draw all the defenders' remaining trumps immediately, when you regain the lead.

Again the contract is 4♠ by West. North leads ♣K.

♠ Q J 10 9 8		♠ 7 6 5 4
♥ A J 8 3	N	♥ K Q 7 2
♦ A K	W E	♦ J 8
♣ 7 4	S	♣ A 8 3

Play trumps at trick 2 and lose to ♠A. Regain the lead and play another spade, losing to the ♠K. Keep playing trumps until the defenders have no more. You want to avoid any of your top heart winners being ruffed.

lead towards high cards

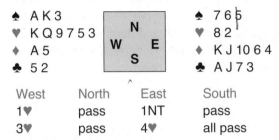

	♠ A K 3		♠ 7 6 5
	♥ K Q 9 7 5 3		♥ 8 2
	♦ A 5		♦ K J 10 6 4
	♣ 5 2		♣ A J 7 3

West	North	East	South
1♥	pass	1NT	pass
3♥	pass	4♥	all pass

Contract 4♥ by West. North leads ♠Q.

You can see one spade and one club loser, but the main problem is to estimate how many hearts will be lost. It could be as many as three if North has ♥A J 10 6 4 but there need only be one trump loser if South has the ♥A and one or two others.

You need to be optimistic and hope South has the ace. Cross to dummy with the ♦K and lead the ♥2. When South plays low, play the ♥K and cross your fingers. It wins! Now cross back to dummy with the ♣A and play the ♥8. If South plays low again, play the ♥Q. But if South plays the ♥A, play a little heart. That way only one heart trick is lost if trumps split 3-2 and ten tricks are won.

draw trumps? – wait awhile

There are many hands when it is right not to draw trumps immediately, as in this example:

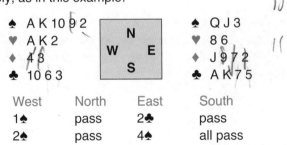

	♠ A K 10 9 2		♠ Q J 3
	♥ A K 2		♥ 8 6
	♦ 4 3		♦ J 9 7 2
	♣ 10 6 3		♣ A K 7 5

West	North	East	South
1♠	pass	2♣	pass
2♠	pass	4♠	all pass

Contract 4♠ by West. North leads ♦A, ♦K and a third diamond.

17

You ruff the third diamond. There are five top spades, two hearts and two clubs. The tenth trick can come from a heart ruff in dummy but this must be done before drawing trumps. Your plan, after ruffing the diamond, should be to play ♥A K and ruff ♥2 with ♠J. Why ♠J rather than ♠3? It's a precaution against an overruff should South have only two hearts.

quiz

Which card would you play as soon as you gain the lead?

```
  ♠ K 6 5 4 3 2        ┌──────┐        ♠ Q J
  ♥ A K 6 3            │   N  │        ♥ Q J 10
  ♦ A                  │ W  E │        ♦ 10 9 7 5
  ♣ K 6                │   S  │        ♣ J 8 5 2
                       └──────┘
```

Contract 4♠ by West. North leads ♥9.

Assuming that the ♥10 won trick one, play the ♠Q (or ♠J). You hope to make five trump tricks, four hearts and one diamond. Draw trumps so that no heart winners get ruffed.

```
  ♠ A K 7              ┌──────┐        ♠ 10 4
  ♥ K Q J 10 6 2       │   N  │        ♥ 9 5
  ♦ A 7                │ W  E │        ♦ 9 8 6 5
  ♣ 5 4                │   S  │        ♣ A 7 6 3 2
                       └──────┘
```

Contract 4♥ by West. North leads ♦K.

Win ♦A. Play ♠A then the ♠K. You can count nine winners and need to make the tenth by trumping ♠7 with ♥9 (for safety). If you play a trump, a defender might win ♥A and play another heart preventing the ruff.

♠ A 7
♥ K 6
♦ J 10 9 4 3
♣ A Q J 10

| N |
| W E |
| S |

♠ 10 8 6 2
♥ A 7 4
♦ A Q 2
♣ K 9 8

Contract 6♦ by West. North leads ♣K.

Win the ♣A and play ♦J (or ♦10 or ♦9). There is no reason to delay drawing trumps but you have to hope that North holds the ♦K and the finesse wins.

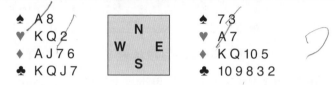

♠ A 8
♥ K Q 2
♦ A J 7 6
♣ K Q J 7

| N |
| W E |
| S |

♠ 7 3
♥ A 7
♦ K Q 10 5
♣ 10 9 8 3 2

Contract 6♣ by West. North leads ♠K.

Win ♠A and play ♥2 to ♥A. East's ♠7 must be discarded urgently before clubs are played. Three rounds of hearts allow ♠7 to be discarded. Then play ♣K to drive out ♣A.

♠ K 7 6 4 2
♥ A
♦ J 10 9 4 3
♣ A J

| N |
| W E |
| S |

♠ A J 9 8 3
♥ 9 2
♦ A Q 2
♣ K 9 8

Contract 6♠ by West. North leads ♦5.

You should play ♦A on the first trick since ♦5 looks very like a singleton and then lead ♠3 to ♠K in case North holds ♠Q 10 5. What if South holds ♠Q 10 5? Too bad! There is nothing you can do about it.

5 count losers – discard them?

Take another look at this quiz question from the previous chapter.

```
        ♠ A 8                            ♠ 7 3
        ♥ K Q 2          N               ♥ A 7
        ♦ A J 7 6    W       E           ♦ K Q 10 5
        ♣ K Q J 7        S               ♣ 10 9 8 3 2
```

Contract 6♣ by West. North leads ♠K.

You have enough winners to make the slam: one spade, three hearts, four diamonds and four clubs (after losing to ♣A) gives twelve tricks. After North has led ♠K, there are two potential tricks to lose: ♣A and a spade. Playing on hearts before trumps enables you to throw away the losing spade and make twelve tricks.

You need to know where your tricks are coming from, so you need to count both your sure winners and your possible winners. However, it is particularly important in a suit contract also to count your losers and your possible losers.

What do we mean by losers? They are those tricks that will, or may, be lost either immediately or later in the play. Counting winners plus losers is a combined exercise and . . .

The count of winners + losers does not always add up to thirteen.

In the last example the total was 14. In the next it is 15.

```
        ♠ K Q J 10 9                     ♠ 8 7 6 4
        ♥ 9              N               ♥ A K Q
        ♦ K 10 4 3 2  W       E          ♦ A Q J
        ♣ A 7            S               ♣ 9 6 2
```

Contract 6♠ by West. North leads ♣K.

You have a surfeit of winners: four spades (after losing to ♠A), three hearts, five diamonds and ♣A. After the ♣K lead, there are two immediate losers. ♠A and a club. If you play a trump, opponents will win their two tricks.

Had North led another suit, there would be one certain loser (♠A) and one potential loser (♣7). However, there would be no need to worry about the potential club loser because there are enough winners to discard it.

The club lead has established a club winner for the defence and something must be done about it before the defence regains the lead. You cannot play a trump at trick two because your priority must be to get rid of that losing club. After winning ♣A, and before playing trumps, you must play two top hearts, discarding ♣7.

needs must

Sometimes a risk needs to be taken since a loser must be discarded urgently.

♠ A 4 2		♠ 8 7 3
♥ 5	N	♥ A Q 7
♦ K Q J 10 9	W E	♦ 8 7 6 2
♣ A K Q J	S	♣ 10 9 8

Contract 5♦ by West. North leads ♠K.

How would you have played if East's hearts had been ♥A K 7? That's easy. You would play the ♥A K and throw a spade away before playing trumps.

With ♥A Q 7 you must play to discard a spade but now some luck is required. You need North to hold ♥K and, at trick two, you lead ♥5 from hand and play the ♥Q from dummy. If ♥Q wins the second trick, a spade is discarded from your hand on ♥A. If it loses, you go down having made the best play.

loser or winner?

The combination of counting both winners and losers before playing to trick one may therefore need to include potential winners and potential losers.

♠ 3 2   [▭▭▭▭▭▭]   ♠ K 4

This suit may provide one winner (if North has ♠A) or two losers (if South has ♠A). First, be pessimistic; assume that you have two losers in the suit and, if you cannot afford them, look to see if you can dispose of one or both of them. If, however, your count of winners means that you need a trick from this suit, you have to be optimistic and presume that North has ♠A. At some stage in the play, you will probably have to lead towards that ♠K 4 holding.

The same situation applies with another finesse position:

♥ 3 2   [▭▭▭▭▭▭]   ♥ A Q

First you should assume that South holds ♥K and that ♥Q is a loser but if that gives you no play for the contract, assume that North holds ♥K and that it is a winner. Let's put the position in context:

♠ A K Q J 10		♠ 8 5 4 3 2
♥ 3 2	**N**	♥ A Q
♦ A K Q	**W E**	♦ 4 3
♣ J 10 3	**S**	♣ 9 8 7 6

Contract 4♠ by West. North leads ♥5.

North's lead has forced you to make an immediate decision. Well . . . not 'immediate' since you should, as always, take time to consider your plan before playing a card to the first trick.

How many winners? Nine. A tenth if North has ♥K and the finesse is taken. How many losers? Three clubs but another if South has ♥K and the finesse is taken.

Should you count ♥Q as a winner or a loser? No contest . . . it's a loser because there is a way to dispose of it and still win ten tricks. You should win dummy's ♥A, draw trumps and play ♦A K Q, discarding ♥Q. The tenth trick will be a heart ruffed in dummy. Conversely:

♠ A K Q J 10	♠ 8 4 3 2
♥ 3 2	♥ A Q 4
♦ A K 4	♦ Q 3 2
♣ 10 4 3	♣ 6 5 2

Contract 4♠ by West. North leads ♠5.

On a heart lead you would have to play North for the ♥K and play ♥Q on the first trick. The actual lead permits you to play around a little. You should draw trumps (assume they break 3-1), cash ♦A K Q and lead a club from East's hand. Just maybe, the defenders will take their three club tricks but leave South on lead. If South does hold ♥K, it is now too late to make it. For example this might be the position with four tricks to go:

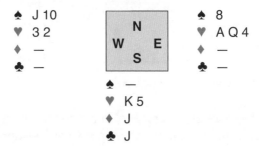

♠ J 10	♠ 8
♥ 3 2	♥ A Q 4
♦ —	♦ —
♣ —	♣ —

♠ —
♥ K 5
♦ J
♣ J

Sometimes the defence slips up, but most of the time you will have to take the heart finesse.

When you need a card to be favourably placed, assume that it is.

quiz

Count your winners/losers and make your plan.

♠ Q 8		♠ A 7 3
♥ K 10 7 6 2	**N**	♥ Q J 4 3
♦ 7	**W** **E**	♦ A K 9
♣ A 7 4 3 2	**S**	♣ 9 8 5

Contract 4♥ by West. North leads ♠6.

There are four possible losers: one spade, one heart and two clubs. There is a temptation to let the lead run to ♠Q (establishing two winners in the suit) but it is far better to discard the spade loser. Win ♠A and play ♦A K, discarding ♠Q. Given normal breaks in hearts and clubs you will make ten tricks, losing one heart and two clubs.

♠ A 4		♠ Q J 3
♥ A 4 3	**N**	♥ 9 7 5
♦ A K 8 7 6 5 4	**W** **E**	♦ Q 3 2
♣ A	**S**	♣ K 9 6 5

Contract 6♦ by West. North leads ♣Q.

There are three possible losers, one spade and two hearts but you can dispose of two of them. One on ♣K and the other on a winning spade in dummy. Win ♣A, cash ♦A K only (even if the suit breaks 3-0) and play ♠A and ♠4. ♠K must be lost but a spade winner is set up in East's hand and ♦Q is the entry to cash the winners. Resist the temptation of the spade finesse, which would mean using the only entry to dummy, ♦Q. If the finesse loses, you cannot get back to the second spade winner.

♠ K		♠ A Q 2
♥ K Q J 10 6 3	**N**	♥ 8 7 4 2
♦ A 7 2	**W** **E**	♦ 6 4 3
♣ 9 6 2	**S**	♣ K Q J

Contract 4♥ by West. North leads ♦K.

♥A and ♣A must be lost and the diamond lead means that there are two diamond losers. You cannot afford to play any trumps because the defenders will take their diamond tricks when you lose the lead. You must get rid of a diamond loser first. Play ♠K, overtake with ♠A and discard a losing diamond on ♠Q.

```
        ♠ A 3 2                        ♠ Q 6
        ♥ A 9 7 4          N           ♥ Q J 10 8 3
        ♦ A 4 2        W       E       ♦ J 8 3
        ♣ A 7 6            S           ♣ 8 3 2
```

Contract 2♥ by West. North leads ♣K.

There are six possible losers: one spade, one heart, two diamonds and two clubs. After winning ♣A, you should immediately try to establish a second spade trick by playing ♠2 towards ♠Q 6. If North has ♠K, there will be time to discard one of East's losers on ♠A. If South's ♠K wins the second trick, your plan should be to ruff a spade in dummy and take the trump finesse. It's a time for optimism.

```
        ♠ A K 8                        ♠ J 4 2
        ♥ A 10 8 7 4 2     N           ♥ J 6 3
        ♦ A Q          W       E       ♦ K J 10 9 6
        ♣ K 3              S           ♣ 4 2
```

Contract 4♥ by West. North leads ♣5.

Thank you, North, for leading a club! It removes the problem of two club losers. Say South wins ♣A and leads a spade. Two trumps and a spade make three possible further losers but you can discard the spade on East's diamonds. Cash ♥A and another heart. A 2-2 break will see you home with an overtrick. If trumps break 3-1, and a spade is led by a defender, you now play on diamonds and hope that the defender with the master trump has at least two diamonds. A spade is thrown on the third diamond and, if it is ruffed, you don't care since it is with your second trump loser.

6 count losers – trump them?

Different declarers count losers in different ways.

```
♠ A K Q J 10          N          ♠ 8 7 6
♥ A K 3          W    E          ♥ 10 9
♦ K 4 3               S          ♦ A Q J
♣ A 7                            ♣ 9 6 4 3 2
```

Contract 6♠ by West. North leads ♣K.

There is one unavoidable club loser. Do you count ♥3 as a second potential loser but then appreciate that it can be eliminated by ruffing it in dummy? Or, when you count your winners (and arrive at eleven top winners) do you count ♥3 as the required extra winner because it can be ruffed in dummy?

It really doesn't matter how you think as long as you keep a trump in dummy, either to ruff that ♥3 as a loser or make it into a winner by ruffing it. You must draw just two rounds of trumps before playing ♥A K 3.

You avoid having that heart loser because you can trump it, but you also gain an extra winner by so doing. That extra trick comes only because you trumped in the hand with the shorter trumps.

Remember, you should count your winners and losers from the viewpoint of the hand which has the longer trump suit.

For example:

```
♠ A 9 8 7             N          ♠ K Q J 10 3
♥ K Q J          W    E          ♥ 10 6 3 2
♦ A J 9 2             S          ♦ K 4 3
♣ A 2                            ♣ 4
```

Contract 6♠ by West. North leads ♣K.

If you count from the West viewpoint, there is a chance that you may come to the wrong conclusion. There are five spade winners, three heart winners (after losing to ♥A), two diamond winners and one club winner.

Can the twelfth trick be made by trumping ♣2 in dummy? No! Trumping in the East hand reduces the spade winners from five to four. The ♣2 is not a loser, but neither is it a winner.

Trumping in the hand with the fewer trumps gains a trick. Trumping in the hand with the longer trumps does not usually produce an extra trick.

There should be no problem if counting winners and losers is done from the viewpoint of the hand with the longer trumps. Here it is East and it is clear that diamonds must provide three winners and no losers. So the diamond finesse will have to be taken.

You may, initially, count a possible loser in diamonds. When you count winners you realise instead that you must rely on ♦J being an additional winner because the ♥A is an inescapable loser.

Counting the losers that would remain AFTER drawing trumps is a useful guide to planning the play.

is there time to ruff a loser?

When you recognise that there is one loser too many, you may not be able to ruff it or discard it straightaway. You may need to make a plan to ruff it eventually in the hand with the shorter trumps.

	♠ A Q 10 9 3		♠ K J 6
	♥ 10 4 3	N	♥ 8 2
	♦ A 5	W E	♦ K 7 4 2
	♣ K 8 4	S	♣ A 7 5 2

How do you play 4♠ if North leads ♦Q?

The winners are five spades, two diamonds and two clubs. The losers, after drawing trumps, are three hearts and a club.

Nothing can be done about that club loser but maybe a heart loser can be ruffed in dummy.

Make your plan. Win ♦A and play a heart immediately. Win the return and play another heart. Win the next trick and trump the final heart in dummy. Even if the defence switches to trumps at trick three, there will still be a trump left in dummy to ruff the heart.

You make five spades, four outside top winners and that vital ruff in East's hand.

♠ A Q 10 9 3		♠ K J 6
♥ 10 4 3	N	♥ 8 2
♦ A 5	W E	♦ K 7 4 2
♣ K 8 4	S	♣ A 7 5 2

How do you play 4♠ if North leads ♣2?

This is the same hand but North has found a good lead. A club must still be lost, but you won't be able to ruff a heart if the defence keep leading trumps.

The trump lead puts the defence a step ahead. If you play a heart at trick two, the defence can lead another spade. A second round of hearts will be won by the defender with the outstanding trump and no doubt the third spade would be played. This removes the third trump in dummy and stops your last heart being ruffed.

Another plan is needed. Play a heart at trick two, giving the defence a chance to go wrong. But if they play another trump, you will have to try the club suit for the tenth trick hoping that clubs break 3-3 and that East's fourth club becomes a winner.

Before the ♠K has gone from dummy (so that the defence cannot take its third heart trick), a small club should be played from both hands. It may seem odd but it is better to lose the first trick in the suit where you need to lose a trick, as you keep better control.

Suppose the defence cashes its second heart winner and then plays the third trump. This is the position after you have won three tricks and lost three tricks:

	♠ A Q		♠ —
	♥ 10		♥ —
	♦ A 5		♦ K 7 4 2
	♣ K 8		♣ A 7 4

There are four clubs still outstanding. If they break 2-2, East's ♣7 is a winner and your losing heart can be discarded on it.

It is usually a good idea to delay playing the critical suit (clubs in this example) until the last moment. Take the other certain winners first. Here, you could play ♦A, ♦K, trump a diamond and cash ♠A. It gives the chance for a defender to make a helpful club discard.

> Defenders sometimes have a problem when they are forced to discard and may throw a card that helps declarer.

avoid being overtrumped

As well as counting the number of trumps held by the defenders, you should know how big they are. You may need to ruff with a high trump to avoid an overruff.

On the next example, declarer was so thankful that his opponents had not found the killing defence that he gave them a gift in return.

	♠ A 7 6		♠ 9 8
	♥ Q J 10 9 6		♥ A K 3
	♦ Q 2		♦ 10 9 8
	♣ A 8 7		♣ K 6 4 3 2

Contract 4♥ by West.

North led ♦A and continued with ♦3. South won with ♦K and returned ♦J.

The defence had chances at tricks one, two and three to beat the contract. A spade switch at any time would have set up a spade winner for the defence before declarer had time to draw trumps and establish winners in the club suit (by playing a small club from both hands).

Sadly West trumped the third round of diamonds with ♥6 and North overtrumped with ♥7. Even if the hearts split 4-1, West can afford to ruff with a bigger heart. A club can be given up before drawing the trumps and then East can overruff North if South wins the club and leads another diamond.

This was the full hand:

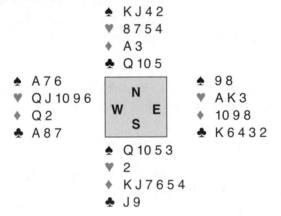

```
                    ♠ K J 4 2
                    ♥ 8 7 5 4
                    ♦ A 3
                    ♣ Q 10 5
   ♠ A 7 6          ┌─────────┐        ♠ 9 8
   ♥ Q J 10 9 6     │    N    │        ♥ A K 3
   ♦ Q 2            │ W     E │        ♦ 10 9 8
   ♣ A 8 7          │    S    │        ♣ K 6 4 3 2
                    └─────────┘
                    ♠ Q 10 5 3
                    ♥ 2
                    ♦ K J 7 6 5 4
                    ♣ J 9
```

Don't send a boy to do a man's job

quiz

Count your winners and losers and make your plan.

♠ A 9 4 3			♠ 2
♥ A K Q 9 7		N	♥ J 10 4
♦ J 3	W	E	♦ 8 7 5 4 2
♣ A 3		S	♣ K 9 7 2

Contract 4♥ by West. North leads ♦A K Q. South discards spades on the second and third round of diamonds.

Your two small spades will have to be ruffed in dummy if the contract is to be made. Whilst it is normal to draw trumps as soon as possible, to prevent the defenders ruffing your winners, here drawing trumps must wait.

You ruffs ♦Q, plays ♠A and another spade ruffing with ♥10. Your hand is re-entered by playing ♥4 to ♥A and the third spade is ruffed with ♥J. As South discarded two spades on the diamonds, there is a chance that he could overruff dummy, but by trumping with ♥J and ♥10 the threat is eliminated.

Only when both spades are ruffed can you draw the rest of the trumps. Because of the two ruffs in the short trump hand, the contract makes with one spade, two clubs and seven heart tricks.

♠ A 8 5			♠ 9 7 3
♥ K J 9 8		N	♥ Q 10 7 3 2
♦ A K	W	E	♦ 10 9 4
♣ J 7 4 3		S	♣ A 8

Contract 3♥ by West. North leads ♠6.

Count losers as if you were sitting East, the hand with the longer trumps. Two spades, one heart, one diamond and one club make five losers. You can trump the diamond loser in West's hand to get rid of the loser and gain an extra trick.

Win the first trick with ♠A and play a trump. If both hands follow suit you can draw trumps when you get in again and then ruff a diamond with one of West's trumps. Should you find that hearts break 4-0, you should cash ♦A K and ruff a diamond before drawing the remaining trumps.

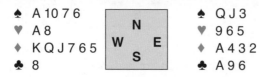

♠ A 10 7 6		♠ Q J 3	
♥ A 8		♥ 9 6 5	
♦ K Q J 7 6 5		♦ A 4 3 2	
♣ 8		♣ A 9 6	

Contract 6♦ by West. North leads ♥K.

Potential losers are a spade and a heart. There are only nine top winners. Spades must provide the extra winners without losing a spade trick.

So South must hold ♠K. Plan to win ♥A, draw all the trumps finishing in dummy and then lead ♠Q. Provided South holds ♠K, twelve tricks will be made – at least three spades, one heart, six diamonds and one club. That comes to eleven and the extra one will be ruffing the fourth spade in East's hand. Note that a spade ruff by East is an extra trick, but a club or heart ruff in West's hand is not.

♠ A J 7 6 5 3		♠ 9 4 2	
♥ K 7		♥ A 9 4 2	
♦ 3		♦ A 9 6 2	
♣ A 8 4 3		♣ K 6	

Contract 4♠ by West. North leads ♦Q.

There is a danger that you could lose two trumps and two clubs. Suppose you won ♦A and played ♠A and another. All would be well if spades broke 2-2 but a 3-1 break means the hand with three trumps would win the second round and play a third, drawing East's last trump.

The plan must be to ruff a club in dummy. Win ♦A and draw just one round of trumps with ♠A. Now you play ♣K, ♣A and trump a club. Come back to hand with a heart and ruff the last club. It doesn't matter if it gets overruffed with one of the opponents' spade winners.

♠ A 9 7
♥ A K Q J 6 5
♦ 7 4
♣ 6 4

♠ 5 3
♥ 9 4 3
♦ A K 9 5 3
♣ K 5 3

Contract 4♥ by West. North leads ♣Q.

Play low on the lead. North won't have led the ♣Q from an A Q J holding. You will always lose two club tricks unless South has a singleton ♣A. You must take care not to lose two spades as well.

No problem, you can trump a spade in dummy. When you gain the lead, you should cash only one top trump before playing ♠A and another spade. A spade trick has to be lost before one can be ruffed. If you play two top trumps before giving up a spade, you might find the trumps break 3-1 and the opponent winning the spade will play a third heart.

♠ A 4 2
♥ A K Q 7 3
♦ 5 4 3
♣ K 6

♠ 7
♥ J 10
♦ J 8 7 6 2
♣ A Q J 10 2

Contract 4♥ by West. North leads ♠K.

Do not consider using East's trumps to ruff the losing spades. You need them to help you draw trumps You can cope even with a 5-1 break as you have the five top hearts.

There are enough tricks without any ruffing. You should win ♠A, take two rounds of trumps with ♥J 10, play ♣2 to ♣K, draw the remaining trumps and cash your club winners. You will make an overtrick.

7 danger – don't squander trumps

Trumping in the hand that has the fewer trumps will gain an extra trick. Trumping in the hand with the longer trumps may be necessary or tactically desirable, but it does not automatically provide an extra trick. Therefore . . .

> Do not trump in the hand with longer trumps without good reason. On many hands, it endangers the contract to do so.

How would you plan the play on this hand?

♠ 4		♠ A 7 3
♥ K J 7	**N**	♥ Q 6 5
♦ A K Q J 2	**W E**	♦ 7 4 3
♣ K J 7 2	**S**	♣ Q 10 6 4

Contract 5♦ by West. North leads ♠K.

The game in diamonds is much better than 3NT, where you would lose too many spade tricks.

After you win dummy's ♠A, you might be tempted to score your lowly ♦2 by ruffing one of East's spades. Do not succumb! It may not seem to matter but you would be reducing the number of trumps in the hand with the longer holding.

Only a 5-0 diamond break would stop ♦2 being a winner in its own right, so there is no need to trump with it – it won't create an extra trick. More importantly, ♦2 will be a protection when you lose the lead to establish your heart and club winners and the defence keep forcing you to ruff spades.

Let's look at the complete deal and see what might happen if you trump a spade at trick two.

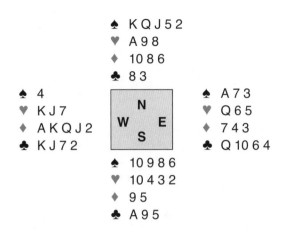

You win ♠A and trump ♠3 with ♦2. You have two losers, ♥A and ♣A , and there are enough winners after the two missing aces have been driven out. You draw trumps, North has three and South discards ♣5 on the third round. You have won the first five tricks and this is the position:

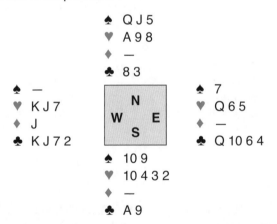

You have to drive out ♣A, so you lead ♣2 to ♣10. South wins ♣A and leads ♠10. You have to trump this with ♦J and you cash the three established club winners. You have now won nine tricks and lost just ♣A, so everyone has three cards:

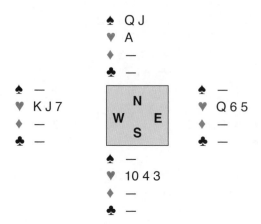

You play a heart. North wins and cashes two spades – two down.

Let's go back. You did NOT ruff a spade at trick two. Draw trumps and drive out the ♣A. This is the position:

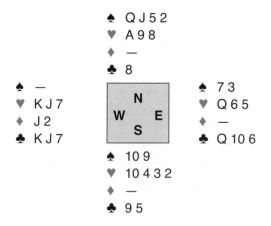

South leads ♠10. You trump with ♦2. You still have ♦J to trump another spade when you drive out ♥A. Contract made.

Good opponents know that you may run out of trumps. They may make you ruff every time they gain the lead, to shorten your trumps till you run out of them. This tactic is called a 'forcing' defence.

If you run out of trumps your contract may go down. Don't help the defence by forcing yourself voluntarily.

foresee the danger

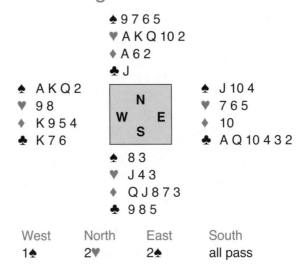

♠ 9 7 6 5
♥ A K Q 10 2
♦ A 6 2
♣ J

♠ A K Q 2
♥ 9 8
♦ K 9 5 4
♣ K 7 6

N
W   E
S

♠ J 10 4
♥ 7 6 5
♦ 10
♣ A Q 10 4 3 2

♠ 8 3
♥ J 4 3
♦ Q J 8 7 3
♣ 9 8 5

West	North	East	South
1♠	2♥	2♠	all pass

North leads ♥A K Q.

If you ruff the ♥Q, you reduce your trumps to only three. Just because you can ruff does not mean you have to. Simply discard ♦4 on ♥Q leaving North on lead. If he plays another heart you can trump with dummy's ♠10. You can then draw four rounds of trumps using dummy's ♠J and your ♠A K Q. Then cash the club winners throwing all the rest of your diamonds away.

The contract fails if you ruff the third round of hearts since North would be left with more trumps than you. This is fairly easy to foresee since it is more likely that the six outstanding trumps will divide 4-2 rather than 3-3. By refusing to ruff, you keep control of the trump suit.

Just because you can trump does not, necessarily, mean that you should. Consider the alternative of discarding in order to keep in control.

keeping trump control

Sometimes the need to keep trump control comes later in the play.

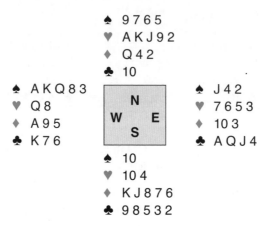

```
                    ♠ 9 7 6 5
                    ♥ A K J 9 2
                    ♦ Q 4 2
                    ♣ 10
    ♠ A K Q 8 3        N        ♠ J 4 2
    ♥ Q 8                       ♥ 7 6 5 3
    ♦ A 9 5       W       E     ♦ 10 3
    ♣ K 7 6           S         ♣ A Q J 4
                    ♠ 10
                    ♥ 10 4
                    ♦ K J 8 7 6
                    ♣ 9 8 5 3 2
```

Contract 4♠ by West. North leads ♥A K and an inspired ♥2 at trick 3.

When you count winners and losers, all looks well. There are ten top winners and only three losers. On ♥A K, South follows with ♥10 4 (to show a doubleton) and he ruffs ♥2. It looks safe to overruff and start drawing trumps . . . but is it? South discards ♣2 on ♠A and this is the position:

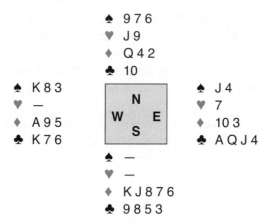

```
                    ♠ 9 7 6
                    ♥ J 9
                    ♦ Q 4 2
                    ♣ 10
    ♠ K 8 3            N        ♠ J 4
    ♥ —                         ♥ 7
    ♦ A 9 5       W       E     ♦ 10 3
    ♣ K 7 6           S         ♣ A Q J 4
                    ♠ —
                    ♥ —
                    ♦ K J 8 7 6
                    ♣ 9 8 5 3
```

Because trumps break 4-1 a trump trick has been created for North. The contract must now fail and if North ruffs the third round of clubs it goes two down.

You can counter this expert defence by discarding a diamond on the third heart and winning whatever South leads to trick four. You can now draw trumps and take the remaining tricks.

quiz

♠ A K Q 10 8		♠ J 9
♥ A K 4 3	N	♥ Q J 10
♦ Q 4	W E	♦ A 9 7 6 3
♣ Q 10	S	♣ 7 6 4

Contract 4♠ by West. North leads ♣A K J. South follows to all three clubs.

Can you see how you might make this contract even if the trumps break 5-1?

On normal distribution, you have ten winners and only three losers.

You could trump ♣J, draw trumps in four rounds and thereafter make four top hearts plus ♦A. That comes to ten tricks.

The only danger here is that trumps split 5-1. This is unlikely but you can guard against it by refusing to trump ♣J and discarding a losing diamond instead. A fourth round of clubs would be ruffed in dummy. West's five spades are retained to draw trumps if they split that badly.

Only if South were void in one of the red suits would this tactic fail.

8 there is no 'short' hand

So far one hand has had fewer trumps (the 'short' hand) than the other (the 'long' hand). You use the trumps in the short hand to make extra tricks. But often both hands have an equal number of trumps. What now?

The answer is that you assign one of those hands as the short hand – pick the one in which extra tricks can be made by trumping. The other hand then becomes the long hand, which will be used to draw the opposition's trumps. The short hand can be either dummy or declarer. The natural inclination is to make additional tricks by trumping in dummy but, with equal length in trumps, ruffing in declarer's hand is just as effective.

♠ A K 4 2		♠ Q J 10 9
♥ A 2	N	♥ K 5 4
♦ A 7 2	W E	♦ K Q J
♣ K 8 7 3	S	♣ A 5 4

Contract 6♠ by West. North leads ♥Q.

Apart from a very unlikely 5-0 trump split the contract is unbeatable. It is declarer's hand, which will become the short hand because it has the ability to make an extra trick by ruffing.

Win the first trick with ♥A and play ♠A and ♠2 (you want to retain ♠K). South shows out on the second round of spades, but the 4-1 break won't hurt. You continue with ♥K and ♥4 and ruff with ♠K. You can afford to do this as you have all the high trumps and you avoid being overruffed.

Now draw the remaining trumps and cash the five top winners in diamonds and clubs to give the required twelve tricks. This line is far better than the only alternative, which is to draw trumps and hope that clubs break 3-3.

the cross-ruff

Sometimes there are hands where the distribution allows for ruffing alternately in both the declarer and the dummy hands. They are often hands where the quality of the combined trump suit is poor.

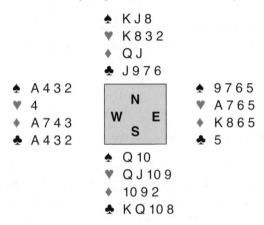

```
              ♠ K J 8
              ♥ K 8 3 2
              ♦ Q J
              ♣ J 9 7 6
♠ A 4 3 2        N        ♠ 9 7 6 5
♥ 4           W     E     ♥ A 7 6 5
♦ A 7 4 3        S        ♦ K 8 6 5
♣ A 4 3 2                 ♣ 5
              ♠ Q 10
              ♥ Q J 10 9
              ♦ 10 9 2
              ♣ K Q 10 8
```

Contract 2♠ by West. North leads ♦Q.

Use a pack of cards to make up the deal. Try the effect of winning ♦A and then trumping everything in sight: ♣A and club ruff; ♥A and heart ruff; club ruff and so on. You should end up having made the five top winners that were obvious at the outset plus three tricks by ruffing hearts and another three by ruffing clubs. A total of eleven tricks!

Of course, it is not suggested that East/West ought to be in game. Just 2♠ is probably right, but, in this example, the distribution in the suits is particularly suitable.

There is one, seemingly small, point to note. After all the cross-ruffing took place, ♠A and ♦K were the two top winners left. ♦K was not needed as an entry to dummy and, therefore, it is a good idea to cash it early, say at trick two. It was not vital to cash the side suit winner early in this hand but it is on the next.

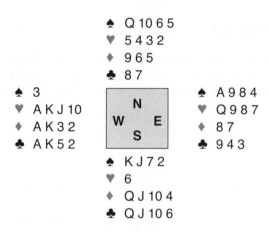

　　　　　　♠ Q 10 6 5
　　　　　　♥ 5 4 3 2
　　　　　　♦ 9 6 5
　　　　　　♣ 8 7

♠ 3　　　　　　　　　　　♠ A 9 8 4
♥ A K J 10　　　　　　　♥ Q 9 8 7
♦ A K 3 2　　　　　　　 ♦ 8 7
♣ A K 5 2　　　　　　　 ♣ 9 4 3

　　　　　　♠ K J 7 2
　　　　　　♥ 6
　　　　　　♦ Q J 10 4
　　　　　　♣ Q J 10 6

Contract 6♥ by West. North leads ♥2.

There are only nine top tricks but the distribution is ideal for a cross-ruff. If the three remaining trumps in both the East and West hands can be made separately, that will add three tricks to the tally of winners. The fact that all the trumps in the East/West hands rank higher than any held by the defence is a bonus. There can be no overruffs.

Suppose you win the first trick in hand and play ♠3 to ♠A and ruff a spade. You cash ♦A K and ruff a diamond. Another spade ruff is followed by a diamond ruff and East's last spade is ruffed. Nine tricks have been won and this is the position:

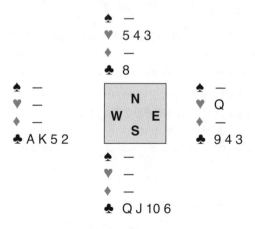

　　　　　　♠ —
　　　　　　♥ 5 4 3
　　　　　　♦ —
　　　　　　♣ 8

♠ —　　　　　　　　　　♠ —
♥ —　　　　　　　　　　♥ Q
♦ —　　　　　　　　　　♦ —
♣ A K 5 2　　　　　　　♣ 9 4 3

　　　　　　♠ —
　　　　　　♥ —
　　　　　　♦ —
　　　　　　♣ Q J 10 6

In theory, you have the required extra three tricks (♣A K and ♥Q). In fact, you have only two (one top club and ♥Q). What has happened is that North has discarded a club when he could not follow to the fourth diamond. You must take your two top club winners early, preferably at tricks two and three, before North is able to discard one.

quiz

Plan the play on this hand

♠ Q J 10 9
♥ A K 3 2
♦ 5
♣ A K 8 4

N
W E
S

♠ A K 8 7
♥ 4
♦ A K 3 2
♣ 7 5 3 2

Contract 6♠ by West. North leads ♠6.

Win the spade lead and cash ♣A K immediately, followed by ♥A K and ♦A K. Now cross-ruff the two hearts and two diamonds. That makes eleven tricks and you still have a spade winner for the twelfth trick.

When the plan is to play a cross-ruff, always cash the top winners in a side suit first (unless they are needed as entries).

9 ruffing in the long hand

You have heard about the benefit of ruffing in the short hand and the potential danger of ruffing in the long hand. This is 'best advice' for most deals, but not always true. There are times when ruffing in the long hand is the best way to go about things!

In this example, the quality of the trump suit is so poor that ruffing with the small trumps is the ideal way of using them.

```
        ♠ K7642                      ♠ A3
        ♥ A432          N            ♥ J76
        ♦ 9         W       E        ♦ A742
        ♣ 986           S            ♣ A432
```

West	North	East	South
pass	pass	1NT	pass
2♣*	pass	2♦	pass
2♠	all pass		

* 2♣ is Stayman, asking about East's majors.

Contract 2♠ by West. North leads ♦K.

Even if trumps divide 3-3, there are only seven tricks available – four trumps and three aces, but you might get home by ruffing as many diamonds as possible. You win ♦A and ruff a diamond, cross to ♠A and ruff another diamond; cross to ♣A and try to ruff the last diamond. If diamonds break 4-4, you make eight tricks – ♦A plus three diamond ruffs, ♣A, ♥A, and ♠A K.

reversing the dummy

Now for something which sounds perverse and requires some mental agility. The long trump hand becomes the short trump hand! This simply means that more tricks can be made by ruffing in the long hand while the short hand has the job of drawing the trumps when the time is right. When declarer has the long trumps, he must consider how he would play the hand as if he was sitting in dummy. Hence, this technique is called a dummy reversal or reversing the dummy.

This is, of course, directly opposite to the advice given about how you should count your losers (i.e. from the viewpoint of the hand with the longer trumps). But you were warned that there would be exceptions! Let's have an exotic example:

♠ A K Q 5 4		♠ J 10 9
♥ A 3 2	N	♥ K Q 10
♦ 2	W E	♦ A 6 5 3
♣ A 8 4 3	S	♣ K Q 2

Contract 7♠ by West. North leads ♠2 and South follows with ♠7.

6♠ would be easy but the Grand Slam is a little ambitious. You can count only twelve top winners. A 3-3 club break could produce the extra trick or maybe the club loser could be ruffed in dummy.

Suppose you cash one more spade, leaving a trump outstanding but keeping a trump in East's hand, and then play three rounds of clubs. If clubs divide 3-3, your ♣8 is a winner; trumps are drawn and you win the remainder. If clubs break 4-2, it may be that the hand that has the doubleton had only two trumps as well and cannot ruff the third round. The ♣8 can now be ruffed with East's outstanding trump.

This sounds a bit dodgy, is there a better line?

Suppose that three ruffs could be made in your hand. The combined trump suit would then make six tricks rather than the obvious five and that would provide the thirteenth trick. Is that possible?

You should overtake dummy's ♠9 to win the opening lead in your own hand and play ♦2 to ♦A and trump ♦3 with ♠4. Play ♠5 to East's ♠J. This will show whether trumps are breaking 3-2 or 4-1. If 4-1, there will be no alternative but to play on clubs as already described.

Assume, however, that both defenders follow to the second round of trumps. This is the position, with the lead in East's hand:

♠ K Q		♠ J
♥ A 3 2	N	♥ K Q 10
♦ —	W　E	♦ 6 5
♣ A 8 4 3	S	♣ K Q 2

A diamond is ruffed with ♠Q, dummy entered with a club and the last diamond is ruffed with ♠K. Finally dummy is entered with a heart and the last trump is drawn whilst you discard a small club. So this possible loser is discarded on a trump.

The time to consider reversing the dummy is when

■ Dummy's trumps are good enough to draw the defenders' trumps.

■ There are sufficient entries to the dummy hand.

■ There is a short side suit in declarer's hand.

■ There is no realistic prospect of making extra tricks any other way.

Sometimes, you need to ruff with a high trump, not just for safety, but to keep a small trump as an entry to dummy.

If there is a choice, prefer to enter dummy in a side suit before using the trump suit. This reduces the chance of a defender discarding in the side suit and then ruffing it when it is needed as an entry to dummy. In the example, the first entry to dummy had to be a trump in case spades split 4-1.

This is not exactly Really Easy play! But it does explain that, while it is usually right to try and make extra tricks by ruffing in the short hand, there are exceptions.

quiz

Which of these three hands would be suitable for a dummy reversal? The contract in all three is 4♥ by West and North leads ♠K. Assume that the opponents' trumps break 3-2.

```
        ♠  2                            ♠  A 8 7 3
        ♥  A Q J 4 2       N            ♥  K 10 9
        ♦  10 8 7 6     W     E         ♦  9 4 3
        ♣  A Q 7          S             ♣  K 4 2
```

This is ideal for reversing the dummy. ♠A is won and a spade ruffed with a top trump. Dummy is entered with ♣K and a second spade is ruffed high; East is entered with a heart and the last spade is ruffed high. West is left with one small trump but East has two to draw the defenders' trumps.

```
        ♠  2                            ♠  A 8 7
        ♥  A Q J 4 2       N            ♥  K 10 9
        ♦  10 8 7 6     W     E         ♦  9 4 3 2
        ♣  A Q 7          S             ♣  K 4 2
```

This hand is not suitable for reversing the dummy as only two spades can be ruffed and no extra trick is gained. Declarer should play on diamonds and will succeed if both red suits break 3-2.

```
        ♠  2                            ♠  A 8 7 6
        ♥  K Q J 10 9     N            ♥  A 8 7
        ♦  10 8 7       W     E         ♦  A 3 2
        ♣  A 8 7 2        S             ♣  K 5 4
```

East's trumps are as good as ♥A K Q so reversing the dummy is the best chance. A spade is ruffed at trick two, dummy entered with a club to ruff another spade and entered again with ♦A to ruff a third spade. ♥K is cashed and ♥Q overtaken to allow East's hand to draw the last trump.

10 establishing extra winners

When declarer has a side suit in which winners need to be established by driving out the defenders' high cards, the process is much the same as in a no trump contract. Except that when playing in no trumps, you must establish your winners before cashing the top tricks in other suits. In a suit contract you must decide whether some or all of the trumps need to be drawn first.

♠ K Q J 6 5		♠ A 4 3 2
♥ 7 6 4 2		♥ A 9 5
♦ K J		♦ Q 10 9 3
♣ A 7		♣ 8 5

Contract 3NT (not the recommended contract!) by West. North leads ♥K.

Or Contract 4♠ by West. North leads ♥K.

Both contracts are pretty secure. Playing in 3NT, declarer, fearing a club switch if he holds up, wins ♥A at trick one and plays diamonds to establish three tricks by driving out the ♦A. The contract will fail only if North has five hearts and ♦A. So would you have preferred to play in 3NT? Certainly not on a club lead!

In 4♠, you have five spade tricks and two aces for certain. Diamonds provide three more tricks once ♦A has been driven out and that suit will also enable you to discard two losers from your hand.

You should win the first trick and draw trumps. But you must use the top spades in your hand, that is the ♠K Q and ♠J if necessary. Since the ♥K lead has removed dummy's other entry, the ♠A is now the only sure entry to dummy.

Suppose you had, carelessly, drawn trumps with ♠A K Q:

```
        ♠  J 6              ┌─────────┐        ♠  4
        ♥  7 6 4            │    N    │        ♥  9 5
        ♦  K J              │ W     E │        ♦  Q 10 9 3
        ♣  A 7              │    S    │        ♣  8 5
                            └─────────┘
```

Now, needing to establish diamond winners, you play ♦K and it wins. You continue with ♦J, which loses to ♦A and the defence is unkind enough to switch to clubs. There are two diamond winners in dummy but no way of getting at them before losing two hearts and a club.

Let's make things slightly more difficult:

```
        ♠  K Q J 6 5        ┌─────────┐        ♠  A 4 3
        ♥  7 6 4 2          │    N    │        ♥  A 9 5
        ♦  K J              │ W     E │        ♦  Q 10 9 3
        ♣  A 7              │    S    │        ♣  8 5 2
                            └─────────┘
```

Contract 4♠ by West. North leads ♥K.

There are still four losers and, if you take the advice of counting them after all the trumps are drawn, you would have to add another heart loser.

What is to be done? Well, take ♥A as before but play just two rounds of trumps, ♠K Q (you are assuming a probable 3-2 split), before starting to establish the diamond tricks.

Say the defenders are on the ball and play ♦A on the second round. If a club is continued, you win ♣A and enter dummy with ♠A, which draws the last trump and puts you in the East hand to cash the diamonds. If defenders continue hearts, they make you ruff in dummy with ♠A. You have to hope that both defenders follow to ♦Q on which you discard ♣7. Now ♣A is the entry to your hand to draw the final trump.

In the first instance you make ten tricks with five spades, one heart, three diamonds and one club. In the second case your winners are five spades, two hearts (♥A and a heart ruff), two diamonds and ♣A.

Try this:

♠ 9 4	**N**	♠ 8 7 6
♥ A K Q J 10 9 3	**W** **E**	♥ 8 2
♦ 10 8	**S**	♦ K Q 3 2
♣ A 3		♣ Q 10 5 4

Contract 4♥ by West.

North leads ♠3 to South's ♠A, North wins the spade return and plays a third spade.

Although you can quickly see that you are going to lose two spade tricks and will trump the third round, you should make your plan before you play a card from dummy to the first trick. Take time to do this even when no immediate decision is required.

You are about to lose two spades. ♦A is another certain loser and there could also be a club loser. You have only eight top winners plus another that can be established in diamonds. You must get rid of one loser, ♣3, by establishing an extra winner.

You cannot look to the clubs for an extra trick because one must be lost and you cannot afford that. Therefore you must assume that North has ♦A and, if you lead towards ♦K Q twice, you will win both ♦K and ♦Q.

Suppose you draw trumps first and then play a small diamond from hand. Maybe North will be kind enough to go up with ♦A. What if he does not? You win the ♦K but the only entry back to your hand is ♣A and that sets up a club winner for the opposition. So you must play on diamonds before you draw any trumps, which allows you to return to your hand with a trump to play the second diamond.

Suppose North wins the second diamond, how can you get to dummy to make that winning diamond? Go back to trick three. Your planning should make you realise that you must trump North's spade with a big heart. Then you can get to dummy by playing ♥3 to ♥8. If you are careless enough to use ♥3 to ruff the third spade, there is no way of getting to dummy to make that winning diamond.

With long strong trumps never ruff with a small trump when you can afford a big one. It is not only a protection against an overruff but, as here, the small trump may be a vital entry to dummy.

two chances

Here is another example when preserving entries is critical.

♠ 9 4		♠ 8 7 6
♥ A K Q J 10 8 3	N	♥ 9 2
♦ A Q	W E	♦ 8 7 4 2
♣ A 3	S	♣ Q 6 5 4

Again the contract is 4♥ and three rounds of spades are led. This time you have two possible ways of making the extra trick. Either North has ♣K and East's ♣Q will win a trick or South has ♦K and the ♦Q will win a trick when the finesse is taken.

You can try both. Again the key play is to preserve that ♥3 as an entry to dummy.

Ruff the spade with a high heart and immediately play ♣A and ♣3. If South wins ♣K, he will probably lead another club. This must also be trumped with a high heart. Now you can play ♥A and ♥3 to ♥9 and take the diamond finesse.

staying a step ahead

Sometimes establishing tricks in a side suit has to be done before drawing trumps. Perhaps because you need to get rid of a loser quickly. Perhaps because entries to dummy are limited.

♠ K Q J 10		♠ 9 8 7 6
♥ A J 10	N	♥ 7 4 2
♦ A K 3	W E	♦ 8 7 6
♣ 4 3 2	S	♣ A K 5

Contract 3♠ by West. North leads ♣Q.

Here, there is a sure loser in each suit, with a danger of two losers in hearts. There are no discards but there is a 75% chance of success with the double heart finesse. Hearts must be led twice towards your ♥A J 10, finessing both times unless South produces ♥K or ♥Q.

This play needs two entries to dummy. So, you must win the first trick and immediately take the first heart finesse (♥2 to ♥10). North is likely to win this trick and lead another club. Now the second heart finesse is taken. The contract fails only if North has ♥K Q or somebody gets a ruff.

On the next hand, declarer needs to establish an outside trick before being forced in the long trump hand.

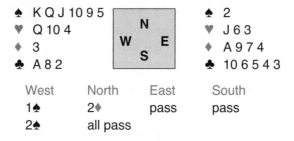

	♠ K Q J 10 9 5		♠ 2
	♥ Q 10 4		♥ J 6 3
	♦ 3		♦ A 9 7 4
	♣ A 8 2		♣ 10 6 5 4 3

West	North	East	South
1♠	2♦	pass	pass
2♠	all pass		

Contract 2♠ by West. North leads ♦K.

Declarer needs to establish a heart trick to make his contract. The danger is that, if spades are played first, you may run short of trumps by having to ruff diamonds.

After winning the first trick, a heart should be played. The defence will lead another diamond, which you ruff to play another heart to drive out the second top honour. No doubt, yet another diamond must be ruffed but you cash ♣A and the third heart. Eight tricks are made – one club, one diamond, one heart and five spades (two by ruffing diamonds and three from the remaining ♠K Q J 10).

How can an inexperienced declarer recognise the need to play on hearts immediately? Firstly, he knows of the danger when the long trumps get shortened. Secondly, he knows that the defence is going to play diamonds at him when he loses the lead. Thirdly, his count of winners will show that he needs to establish one heart trick.

If keeping trump control may be a problem, establish tricks in a side suit early in the play.

This might be the full deal:

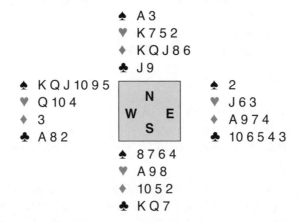

♠ A 3
♥ K 7 5 2
♦ K Q J 8 6
♣ J 9

♠ K Q J 10 9 5   ♠ 2
♥ Q 10 4   ♥ J 6 3
♦ 3   ♦ A 9 7 4
♣ A 8 2   ♣ 10 6 5 4 3

♠ 8 7 6 4
♥ A 9 8
♦ 10 5 2
♣ K Q 7

What if you decided that it was safe to play a trump at trick two? This position will come about with you on lead having won five of the six tricks so far played:

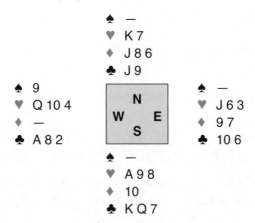

♠ —
♥ K 7
♦ J 8 6
♣ J 9

♠ 9   ♠ —
♥ Q 10 4   ♥ J 6 3
♦ —   ♦ 9 7
♣ A 8 2   ♣ 10 6

♠ —
♥ A 9 8
♦ 10
♣ K Q 7

Three more tricks are needed but only two will materialise. That heart trick will not be made. You lead a heart, South wins and returns ♦10; you ruff but will make only ♣A – seven tricks.

quiz

Plan the play on these hands:

♠ A K J 10 3	♠ Q 4 2
♥ A 7 6	♥ 10 5
♦ A 3	♦ K Q 6 4 2
♣ Q 8 6	♣ 9 7 2

Contract 4♠ by West. North leads ♥K.

You might think of ducking the opening lead. Then you would be able to ruff a heart if North obligingly led another one. But North might lead a club at trick two and the defence could take three top tricks in clubs.

There is a better way. You should assume that spades will break 3-2 and diamonds 4-2. Then you can establish a diamond trick before all the trumps are drawn. Win ♥A, cash just ♠A K and play ♦A, ♦K and trump a diamond with ♠J. East's ♠Q draws the last trump and puts you in the East hand to cash the diamonds.

♠ A 2	♠ 9 8
♥ K 5 3	♥ 7 2
♦ A Q J 10 4 2	♦ K 7 5
♣ A 2	♣ K 8 7 6 5 3

Contract 5♦ by West. North leads ♠K.

The danger is that a spade and two hearts may be losers. South might have ♥A (♥K would become a trick and your third heart could be trumped) but a 3-2 club break offers better prospects.

Win ♠A, cash ♦A Q and then play ♣A, ♣2 to ♣K and ruff a club high. If the clubs break 3-2, the remaining clubs in East's hand are masters and there is ♦K as an entry.

11 creating extra winners

A great thing about playing in a suit contract is that you can 'create' winners which are impossible in a no trump contract. This is much more fun . . . when it works!

	West		East
♠	A K Q J 4	♠	10 9 8
♥	A 4 3 2	♥	J 8 7
♦	J 7	♦	A 5 4 3 2
♣	7 6	♣	A J

Contract 3NT by West. North leads ♣K.

There is no chance of making nine tricks in no trumps. East's 5-card diamond suit cannot be established before the defence takes at least four more club tricks when the lead is lost.

Contract 4♠ by West. North leads ♣K.

4♠ looks pretty hopeless as well. There are four losers – two hearts, one diamond and one club. Count winners – five spades, one heart, one diamond and one club comes to eight. Even if you ruff a heart in East's hand, that would be only one extra trick.

However, in the suit contract, dummy's diamonds might be made into winners. After winning ♣A, you should play a small diamond from both hands. Assume North wins this trick, cashes ♣Q and leads a heart which goes to ♥7, ♥10 and ♥A. The defence has won two tricks and, potentially, established two more in hearts.

However, if spades break 3-2 and diamonds split 3-3, you can make your contract. You cross to ♦A and ruff a diamond with a high spade. Now you draw trumps, ending in East's hand, and with a lucky 3-3 break, all of dummy's remaining diamonds have become good. In total you win five spades, three diamonds, one heart and one club.

The side suit may be in declarer's hand:

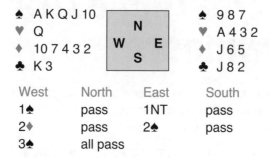

♠ A K Q J 10   ♠ 9 8 7
♥ Q   ♥ A 4 3 2
♦ 10 7 4 3 2   ♦ J 6 5
♣ K 3   ♣ J 8 2

West	North	East	South
1♠	pass	1NT	pass
2♦	pass	2♠	pass
3♠	all pass		

Contract 3♠ by West. North leads ♣10.

No worries. Don't draw trumps yet . . . just play diamonds every time you get the lead. Let the defenders win the three tricks in diamonds, which you can afford. Probably you will end up with two small, but master, diamonds if the suit breaks 3-2. Provided trumps split 3-2, you have no problem with being forced to trump in your hand since East's ♠9 8 7 can ruff the fourth club.

This example may persuade you not to abandon hope even when you arrive in an inferior contract.

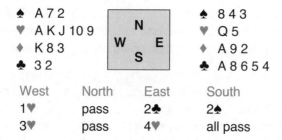

♠ A 7 2   ♠ 8 4 3
♥ A K J 10 9   ♥ Q 5
♦ K 8 3   ♦ A 9 2
♣ 3 2   ♣ A 8 6 5 4

West	North	East	South
1♥	pass	2♣	2♠
3♥	pass	4♥	all pass

Contract 4♥ by West. North leads ♠5.

In 3NT there are nine top tricks. 4♥ is precarious but not hopeless. You can count only nine top winners but the club suit might provide an extra trick. You win ♠A and immediately give up the club trick that you have to lose by playing small from both hands. The defenders will take two spade winners but cannot lead a third round because you can ruff with ♥Q and discard a losing diamond.

Say the defenders exit with a diamond. Win ♦K, cross to ♣A and ruff a club. If clubs are 3-3, draw trumps and enter dummy with ♦A to cash the club winners. If clubs are 4-2 cross to dummy with ♥Q and ruff a club. You are down to three trumps so you hope the opponents' hearts break 3-3.

Let's end with the bizarre in the matter of creating tricks out of nothing. This was actually dealt in real life.

♠ K 10 9 5 4 3 2		♠ A 8 7 6
♥ —		♥ 8 7 6 5 4 3 2
♦ 8 7 4		♦ A
♣ 5 4 2		♣ 3

Contract 6♠ by West. North leads ♠Q and South discards a club.

A wild auction saw South bid to 6♦. This can go down, but West took the precaution of sacrificing in 6♠ which he expected to go down. But as the cards lay, the contract could not be beaten!

West won ♣A, ruffed a heart and cashed ♠K. He crossed to ♦A, ruffed another heart, ruffed a diamond and ruffed a third heart. When the suit broke 3-3, dummy's hearts were good and could be reached with a second diamond ruff. This was the full hand:

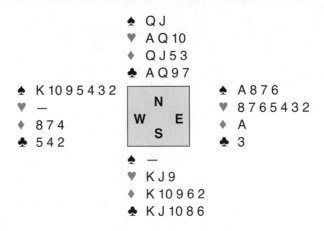

All thirteen tricks made with only eleven high card points. Outrageous fortune . . . but West wasn't satisfied. He thought that he should have been doubled!

quiz

What is the optimum contract on this hand?

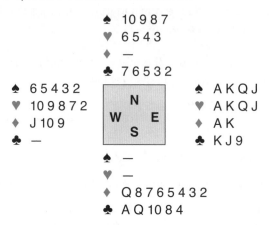

♠ 10 9 8 7
♥ 6 5 4 3
♦ —
♣ 7 6 5 3 2

♠ 6 5 4 3 2
♥ 10 9 8 7 2
♦ J 10 9
♣ —

N
W   E
S

♠ A K Q J
♥ A K Q J
♦ A K
♣ K J 9

♠ —
♥ —
♦ Q 8 7 6 5 4 3 2
♣ A Q 10 8 4

Contract 7♥ by West. North leads ♥3.

Fans of Ian Fleming will probably opt for 7♣ by South which was James Bond's opening bid in *Moonraker*. A scam, of course, intended to relieve East (the villain, Drax) of a considerable sum of money. East makes a penalty double which South redoubles.

7♣ cannot be beaten since two ruffs set up the diamonds and this provides the entries to take two club finesses.

However, suppose that you assume that your partner's double is for take out and bid 7♥? Since South cannot ruff, this makes on a dummy reversal, ruffing three clubs in your hand.

12 the finesse in a suit contract

You know, when taking a finesse, that you are hoping for a specific card to be held by a certain defender. All the most common finesse positions were examined in detail in 'Really Easy Play in No Trumps' and, of course, they apply equally in a suit contract.

However, there are some extra finesses that become available only because there is a trump suit.

the ruffing finesse

Assume that this position has been reached during the play:

```
        ♠ 4
        ♥ A 6              N
        ♦ A 2         W        E
        ♣ 3 2              S
```
```
                           ♠ —
                           ♥ 9
                           ♦ K 5
                           ♣ A Q J 10
```

Spades are trumps and ♠4 is the only one left. You have to win all the remaining tricks to land your contract. The only hope is that North has ♣K: you play a small club and finesse unless North produces ♣K. If the finesse wins, you return to your hand and repeat the finesse and discard the ♥6 loser on ♣A. However . . .

```
        ♠ 4
        ♥ A 6 3            N
        ♦ A 2         W        E
        ♣ 3                S
```
```
                           ♠ —
                           ♥ 9
                           ♦ K 5
                           ♣ A Q J 10
```

You need to make three tricks from the clubs since you have to discard two heart losers. Playing North for ♣K only works if he has ♣K x or ♣K x x since ruffing a third club will bring down the king. However, it is better to play South for ♣K. Now the contract can be made with a ruffing finesse. ♣A is played followed by ♣Q. If South covers with ♣K, it is ruffed by ♠4, dummy is entered with ♦K and your small hearts are discarded on East's master clubs.

If South does not cover, you discard a heart and, providing North cannot win, the lead remains with East and the manoeuvre is repeated. If South still does not cover, the second small heart is discarded; if he does cover, ♣K is ruffed and dummy re-entered with ♦K to take the master club.

There are two points to remember.

- There has to be a second entry to East's hand. Taking the ruffing finesse would be pointless if dummy did not have ♦K.

- If you are certain that North holds ♣K (say he opened 1NT and has to hold ♣K to make up the required points), then you would take the straight finesse and hope that he had ♣K x or ♣K x x.

In other situations the choice of taking a ruffing finesse in preference to a straight finesse may be influenced by the need to prevent one defender from gaining the lead.

	♠ 4 2				♠ —
	♥ K 4 2	N			♥ 5 3
	♦ A 2	W E			♦ K 5 3
	♣ 3	S			♣ A Q J

Again, spades are trumps, ♠4 2 are the only ones that remain and you can afford to lose two tricks. You could choose to play for North to hold ♣K, take the straight finesse and, if it succeeds, discard a heart on ♣A.

However, if the club finesse loses South will probably lead a heart, you will be obliged to put up ♥K and, if North has ♥A, three hearts will be lost.

In fact, the contract is 100% secure if the ruffing finesse is taken. You play a club to ♣A and follow it with ♣Q from dummy. If South covers you ruff, enter dummy with ♦K and throw a heart loser on ♣J. If South plays small, a heart is discarded. Now, if North wins ♣K, the defence can only take one heart straight away and there is time, and the entry, to enjoy East's winning club. The 'safe' hand has been given the lead.

The concept of the 'danger' hand – the one that you want to keep out of the lead – can be as important in a suit contract as it is in no trumps.

taking the right finesse

Sometimes there is a choice of finesses which would not matter in a no trump contract but does in a suit contract. It can offer the opportunity to dispose of a loser.

♠ A K Q J 4			♠ 10 9 6 3
♥ A 7 5	N		♥ 4 3 2
♦ 7 4	W E		♦ A Q J
♣ Q J 10	S		♣ A 7 6

Contract 4♠ by West. North leads ♠2.

First count winners: eight. Two more can be made, by taking finesses, if North has either minor suit king. Alternatively both clubs and diamonds have the potential to make an extra trick even when losing to both kings. That seems fine.

Now count losers (including the possible losers): four. Two hearts plus one diamond and one club if both the finesses are wrong. Not so fine.

Can the number of losers be reduced from four to three? Yes. . . but only if the diamond finesse is taken first. Say trumps are drawn in three rounds and you take the club finesse which loses to South's ♣K. No doubt, he will attack your weak suit, hearts. ♥A is won, the diamond finesse tried but that also loses to South's ♦K and the defence takes two more tricks in hearts.

Now see what happens if the diamond finesse is taken first. It loses to ♦K and South again returns a heart. However, there are two diamond winners established in dummy and a losing heart can be discarded from your hand. The contract makes even though both kings are offside.

With a choice of finesses it is usually right to choose the suit which breaks unevenly. If it fails, the same suit may still provide a discard for a loser.

This example makes the same point:

♠ A K 4 3 2   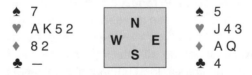   ♠ Q 8 5
♥ 5 4 3   ♥ K Q 2
♦ A K Q   ♦ 6 4 3 2
♣ 6 5   ♣ K Q 2

Contract 4♠ by West. North leads ♦J.

Win the diamond lead and draw three rounds of trumps, which break, to arrive at this position:

♠ 4 3   ♠ —
♥ 5 4 3   ♥ K Q 2
♦ A K   ♦ 6 4 3
♣ 6 5   ♣ K Q 2

You should lead a club, rather than a heart, towards ♣K Q 2. If North has ♣A, two tricks can be made (you return to hand with a diamond to lead the second club) and allows for the discard of a potential heart loser. If a heart is played first, and South wins ♥A, he would be able to establish a second heart trick for the defence while ♣A is still around.

Can you work out the best plan here?

♠ 7   ♠ 5
♥ A K 5 2   ♥ J 4 3
♦ 8 2   ♦ A Q
♣ —   ♣ 4

Trumps (spades) have been drawn, hearts and diamonds have not been played but the defence has a club winner. You need to make six of the last seven tricks.

Count the losers: potentially two: one heart and one diamond (if South has ♦K). Count the winners: five, for certain. Two trumps, made separately, ♥A K and ♦A. The extra trick can come from a diamond finesse (if North has ♦K).

Anything better? Yes! You actually have two finesses on offer. Playing ♥2 towards ♥J 4 3 is also part of the 'finessing' family because you are hoping that a card is well placed: in this case that ♥Q is with North. If you are lucky ♥J becomes the extra trick and, if not, the diamond finesse can still be taken. You double your chances.

the free finesse

Sometimes a defender's lead lets you take a finesse that you are unable, or would not want, to take yourself. If it wins, you gain some advantage but, if it loses you are not disadvantaged.

♠ —		♠ A Q 4 2
♥ A 7 3	**N**	♥ 5 4 2
♦ A Q J 10 3 2	**W E**	♦ K 9
♣ Q J 10 4	**S**	♣ A 9 7 5

Contract 6♦ by West. North leads ♠5.

The contract depends on the club finesse but, if North should happen to have led from a spade holding which includes ♠K, two heart losers could be discarded on ♠A Q. The contract would be safe and the club finesse is then for a possible overtrick. It is a free finesse: play ♠Q at trick one. You expect ♠K from South but, if so, you ruff it and it's back to depending on North having ♣K.

Beware, however:

♠ —		♠ A Q 7 4
♥ A Q 7	**N**	♥ 5 4 2
♦ A Q J 10 2	**W E**	♦ K 9 3
♣ A Q J 10 4	**S**	♣ K 9 7

Contract 6♦ by West. North leads ♠5.

This hand may look similar but, here, the spade finesse on offer has an element of danger. Just suppose this is the complete deal:

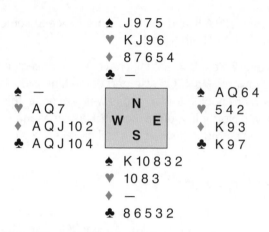

♠ J 9 7 5
♥ K J 9 6
♦ 8 7 6 5 4
♣ —

♠ —
♥ A Q 7
♦ A Q J 10 2
♣ A Q J 10 4

N
W E
S

♠ A Q 6 4
♥ 5 4 2
♦ K 9 3
♣ K 9 7

♠ K 10 8 3 2
♥ 10 8 3
♦ —
♣ 8 6 5 3 2

Contract 6♦ by West. North leads ♠5.

Whatever North leads, there are at least twelve top tricks for the taking. A heart lead would give an overtrick but, otherwise, normal distribution would mean that the heart finesse could be tried later without endangering the contract.

The spade lead seems to offer an extra chance for the overtrick. If North has led away from ♠K, taking the finesse produces the extra trick when North also holds ♥K.

It happens that, by accepting what is a 'Greek gift' rather than a free finesse, the slam will fail. If you ruff, North will make a trump trick; if you discard a heart, North can ruff a club.

It is usually right to assume that you have reached the best contract and to ensure that you make it. Therefore, you should rise with ♠A at trick one. Remember what was said earlier about the danger of trumping in the long hand.

A 'free' finesse may prove to be as costly as a 'free' lunch.

the impossible finesse

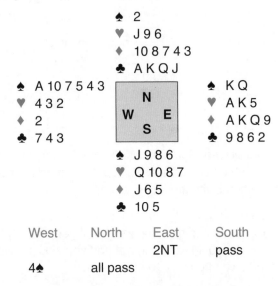

```
              ♠ 2
              ♥ J 9 6
              ♦ 10 8 7 4 3
              ♣ A K Q J
♠ A 10 7 5 4 3              ♠ K Q
♥ 4 3 2          N         ♥ A K 5
♦ 2         W       E      ♦ A K Q 9
♣ 7 4 3          S         ♣ 9 8 6 2
              ♠ J 9 8 6
              ♥ Q 10 8 7
              ♦ J 6 5
              ♣ 10 5
```

West	North	East	South
		2NT	pass
4♠	all pass		

North leads his four top clubs. South discards a heart and a
diamond and declarer trumps the fourth club. When he cashes
♠K Q, North discards ♦3. This is the position:

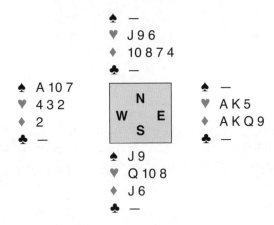

```
              ♠ —
              ♥ J 9 6
              ♦ 10 8 7 4
              ♣ —
♠ A 10 7                   ♠ —
♥ 4 3 2          N         ♥ A K 5
♦ 2         W       E      ♦ A K Q 9
♣ —              S         ♣ —
              ♠ J 9
              ♥ Q 10 8
              ♦ J 6
              ♣ —
```

It looks as though a trump must be lost since East has no spade
to lead for a normal finesse. However, the diamonds will do the
job instead.

♦A is cashed, ♦9 is ruffed. Dummy is entered with ♥A to leave:

♠ A 10		♠ —
♥ 4 3	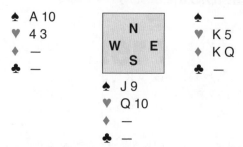	♥ K 5
♦ —		♦ K Q
♣ —		♣ —
	♠ J 9	
	♥ Q 10	
	♦ —	
	♣ —	

When ♦K Q are played, South is caught in a Trump Coup. If he ruffs, you overruff. If South discards, you throw a heart and lead the second diamond with the same result.

Success relied on you ending up with the same number of trumps as South, hence the need to trump that ♦9. If you simply played top winners, South would refuse to ruff and you would have to trump and lead away from ♠A 10 at the end.

This is not dissimilar:

♠ 10		♠ —
♥ 4 3 2	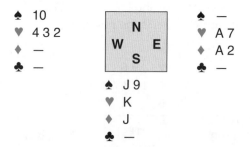	♥ A 7
♦ —		♦ A 2
♣ —		♣ —
	♠ J 9	
	♥ K	
	♦ J	
	♣ —	

With spades as trumps and East on lead, you, needing three tricks, cash the two red suit aces and lead ♦2. South cannot prevent you from winning ♠10. En passant, as they say.

13 leave a trump out?

Suppose this is your trump suit:

♠ A K 7 3   [▭▭▭▭]   ♠ 9 6 4 2

You see a need to draw trumps, cash ♠A K and all players follow suit. There is no point in playing a third round. The defence has to win a trump trick and it matters not when or how they take it.

Allowing a defender to keep the master trump can be advantageous.

```
                        ♠ Q J 8
                        ♥ Q J 10 5
                        ♦ K 10 2
                        ♣ 7 5 4
        ♠ A K 7 6                        ♠ 5 4 3 2
        ♥ K 4 2          N               ♥ 9 8 7
        ♦ Q 8 7      W       E           ♦ J 6 4
        ♣ Q J 6          S               ♣ A K 3
                        ♠ 10 9
                        ♥ A 6 3
                        ♦ A 9 5 3
                        ♣ 10 9 8 2
```

Contract 2♠ by West. North leads ♥Q to ♥A and South returns ♥6.

Whilst you are pleased that the lead has removed the threat of three heart losers, you realise that your problems are not over. Suppose, after winning ♥K, you draw three rounds of trumps. North will take the third round, cash a winning heart and exit, safely, with a club. Three tricks have been lost and, when you have to play the diamonds, you will lose another three.

If, instead, you play just the two top trumps, cash three rounds of clubs and THEN play the third round of trumps, North can cash a heart but then will have to open up the diamonds. You will now make a diamond trick.

Q x x opposite J x x is one of those suits that you want the opponents to lead.

the ruff and discard

In the previous hand, if the play had gone as suggested, North would be faced with losing alternatives. This would be the position after he had been obliged to win his master trump trick.

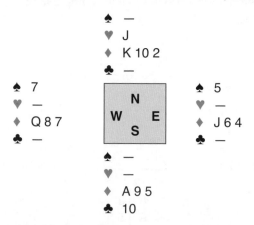

North chose the better, but still losing, alternative by playing a diamond. He could, of course, have played ♥J. This, however, would allow declarer to trump in one hand and discard a losing diamond from the other.

This is an example of a ruff and discard, which, as you can see, produces both an extra trick and eliminates a loser. There will be other examples in a later chapter.

keeping a trump loser in the short hand

When trumps are 5-3, it is again often safe to leave a defender with a master trump to make when he chooses but you should have a reason. Otherwise:

♠ A K 7 6 5		♠ 4 3 2
♥ Q J 4	**N**	♥ A K 3 2
♦ A 4 3	**W E**	♦ 7 6 2
♣ A 2	**S**	♣ 9 6 5

Contract 4♠ by West. North leads ♦K.

Now, if you take just two rounds of trumps before playing hearts and a defender ruffs the third round of hearts, you cannot get at the essential heart winner in dummy because there is no entry to East's hand. You should play ♠A K and a third spade.

Conversely:

♠ A K 9 6 2		♠ 5 4 3
♥ —	**N**	♥ A K Q
♦ A K 2	**W E**	♦ 8 7 6 4
♣ A K Q J 10	**S**	♣ 9 8 7

Contract 6♠ by West. North leads ♦Q.

How annoying to have three winners in dummy but no entry! In fact, provided trumps break 3-2, there is no problem. Cash ♠A K and start taking the club winners. One of two things will happen. The defender with the master spade either ruffs and East's ♠5 becomes an entry or he refuses to ruff and two diamonds are discarded from dummy. You can now ruff your diamond loser.

Recognising the exceptions, it is sometimes good technique to let the defence retain its one master trump.

This is similar:

♠ A K 7 6 5		N		♠ 4 3 2
♥ A Q	W		E	♥ 8 6
♦ A K Q J		S		♦ 4 3 2
♣ A Q				♣ K 7 6 3 2

Contract 6♠ by West. North leads ♠Q.

Only in wonderland do you get dealt this hand but, even there, you wouldn't want the slam to depend on a finesse.

Assuming a 3-2 spade break, there are enough winners on view but there are also two possible losers, one spade and ♥Q. The latter could be thrown on ♣K but there is no outside entry to get to it. You could overtake ♣K to allow a heart finesse to be taken but there is no need to take that chance.

You should win just ♠A K and let a defender retain the master trump. You cash the top diamonds. Let's assume South ruffs the third diamond with the master trump, and returns a heart. You rise with ♥A and carry on with your last diamond winner, throwing a heart from dummy. Now you are able to ruff ♥Q. If nobody ruffs the third diamond, a heart is discarded on the fourth and ♥Q trumped as before.

Find the best line on this hand:

♠ 3		N		♠ A 9 7 5
♥ A K Q J 10	W		E	♥ 4 3 2
♦ J 6 4		S		♦ 10 8 3
♣ A K Q 5				♣ 7 6 2

Contract 4♥ by West. North leads ♦A.

Assume the defence takes three top diamonds and then ♠K is led. There are nine winners but you need one more. If you draw three rounds of trumps, you will need clubs to break 3-3 to make the tenth.

There is an extra chance. Draw just two rounds of trumps and then play the top winners in clubs. If they divide 3-3, simply draw

the final trump and cash ♣5. If they divide 4-2, it is possible that
the hand with the doubleton club also started with only two
trumps. In that case ♣5 will still win a trick because it can safely
be trumped in dummy.

keeping a trump winner in the short hand

One of the obvious reasons for keeping a winning trump in
dummy is that it is required as an entry later in the play.

♠ A K 10 9 2		♠ Q 4 3
♥ A 10 3	N	♥ 5 4 2
♦ K Q	W E	♦ A 7 6 5
♣ Q 7 3	S	♣ K 4 2

Contract 4♠ by West. North leads ♥K.

♣K is not a certain entry to dummy but ♠Q is. You must cash just
♠A K, then unblock ♦K Q before crossing to ♠Q. A heart loser is
discarded on ♦A and clubs will provide the tenth winner in due
course.

The next example is more difficult.

♠ A K J 10 9		♠ Q 4 3
♥ A 10 3	N	♥ 5 4 2
♦ K 8	W E	♦ A 7 6 5 3
♣ K 7 3	S	♣ 8 4

Contract 4♠ by West. North leads ♥6 and South plays ♥Q.

You should win ♥A, not wanting South to switch to a club. There
are two hopes: that diamonds break 3-3 or that South has ♣A.
The chances can be combined but East's trumps are vital for
both. Before drawing any trumps, you should play ♦K, ♦A and
trump a diamond. If diamonds are 3-3, there are two winning
diamonds in dummy, so trumps can now be drawn ending with
East's ♠Q. Two losing hearts can be discarded and a club played
towards ♣K 7 3 for a possible overtrick.

If diamonds are 4-2, you must immediately cross to East's ♠Q and play towards your ♣K 7 3, now hoping that South holds ♣A. If so, either South's ♣A or your ♣K will win this trick and, in either case, there should be time for a losing club to be ruffed in dummy since East still holds ♠4 3.

The first hope was that diamonds split 3-3. The fallback plan relied on South holding ♣A and a kind distribution which allowed a small club to be safely ruffed in the short hand. The ten winners would be: five spades, one heart, two diamonds, ♣K and a club ruff. The three losers would be two hearts and one club.

keeping trump control

On the next hand, dummy's top trump must be retained to prevent the defence from reducing the joint holding.

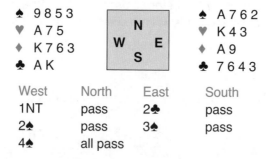

♠ 9 8 5 3		♠ A 7 6 2
♥ A 7 5		♥ K 4 3
♦ K 7 6 3		♦ A 9
♣ A K		♣ 7 6 4 3

West	North	East	South
1NT	pass	2♣	pass
2♠	pass	3♠	pass
4♠	all pass		

Contract 4♠ by West. North leads ♣Q.

With only seven top winners, you will count on a 3-2 spade break for an eighth trick but two more need to be found. Some ruffing will have to be done and it is necessary to keep two spades in both the East and West hands to make the best of this fragile trump holding.

You need to draw just two rounds of trumps but, if you play ♠A and another, the defender with three trumps would probably win and play a third round. The answer is to lead a small spade from both hands, retaining East's ♠A to win the second round of trumps. This would be the position if the defence led a second trump, won by ♠A:

♠ 9 8		♠ 7 6
♥ A 7 5	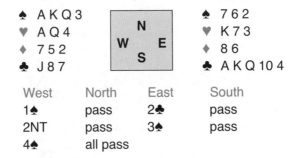	♥ K 4 3
♦ K 7 6 3		♦ A 9
♣ A		♣ 7 6 4

Now you can cash top winners in diamonds and clubs and start cross-ruffing. If there is an overruff, it can only be with the outstanding master trump. At the end of the day, just two spades and one heart will be lost.

What about if North had led ♠K instead?.

The problem is the same and your answer is to let ♠K hold the first trick. Really easy!

quiz

Plan the play on this hand:

♠ A K Q 3		♠ 7 6 2
♥ A Q 4		♥ K 7 3
♦ 7 5 2		♦ 8 6
♣ J 8 7		♣ A K Q 10 4

West	North	East	South
1♠	pass	2♣	pass
2NT	pass	3♠	pass
4♠	all pass		

Contract 4♠ by West. North leads ♠J.

Assume that all the suits break reasonably with trumps being 4-2 and you need to justify your choice of the final contract.

As West, you would be aware that East has just three spades (with four, he would have supported spades immediately). With hindsight, 5♣ looks to be the best contract but difficult to bid. 3NT would fail if the defence were able to take the first five diamond tricks but 4♠ has a good chance of making.

You could bash out ♠A K Q and make twelve tricks provided trumps break 3-3. This is against the odds and you will have four losers if the probable 4-2 spade break occurs.

The clever answer on the lead of ♠J is to follow with ♠2 and ♠3 on the first trick!

Dummy's small trumps protect against losing three diamonds and you can now cope with a 4-2 spade split.

You don't have to win a trick just because you can.

14 the danger hand

The concept of the danger hand is very important when playing in a no trump contract. Usually, it applies when it is known that one hand has established winners and, therefore, needs to be prevented from gaining the lead while declarer goes about his own business of establishing tricks.

However, this suit layout has the potential for three losers whether it is played in no trumps or a suit contract:

♥ A 9 3

♥ K 5 4   ▭   ♥ 8 7 6

♥ Q J 10 2

If South gains the lead, North/South will, immediately, take three heart tricks and, therefore, declarer may be forced to play in such a way as to try to prevent South gaining the lead. For example:

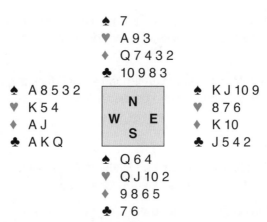

```
              ♠ 7
              ♥ A 9 3
              ♦ Q 7 4 3 2
              ♣ 10 9 8 3
♠ A 8 5 3 2                 ♠ K J 10 9
♥ K 5 4          N          ♥ 8 7 6
♦ A J        W     E        ♦ K 10
♣ A K Q          S          ♣ J 5 4 2
              ♠ Q 6 4
              ♥ Q J 10 2
              ♦ 9 8 6 5
              ♣ 7 6
```

Contract 4♠ by West. North leads ♣10.

Suppose that you win the first trick in hand, cash ♠A and lead another. Sooner or later, South is going to get the lead with the ♠Q to play ♥Q through your king.

You have a discard for one heart loser on the ♣J if you can keep South off lead. You can prevent South gaining the lead by taking the finesse the other way. Cash ♠K and lead ♠J, letting it run if it is not covered. If North happens to have ♠Q x, the cost of the safety play is simply an overtrick.

Let's change the hands slightly with the same contract and lead:

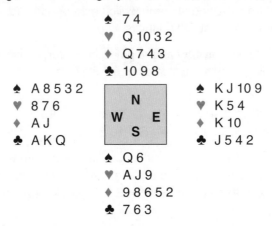

```
              ♠ 7 4
              ♥ Q 10 3 2
              ♦ Q 7 4 3
              ♣ 10 9 8
♠ A 8 5 3 2        N        ♠ K J 10 9
♥ 8 7 6                     ♥ K 5 4
♦ A J         W   E        ♦ K 10
♣ A K Q           S        ♣ J 5 4 2
              ♠ Q 6
              ♥ A J 9
              ♦ 9 8 6 5 2
              ♣ 7 6 3
```

Now it is North that it is the danger hand and it would be right to play ♠A and another at tricks two and three and take the trump finesse.

Again the contract is safe even though an overtrick is given up because one losing heart can be discarded on the fourth club.

loser on loser

Sometimes it is useful to lose a trick by throwing a loser from each hand. This is called a loser on loser play.

Make a plan on the next hand:

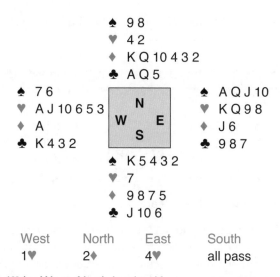

♠ 9 8
♥ 4 2
♦ K Q 10 4 3 2
♣ A Q 5

♠ 7 6
♥ A J 10 6 5 3
♦ A
♣ K 4 3 2

♠ A Q J 10
♥ K Q 9 8
♦ J 6
♣ 9 8 7

♠ K 5 4 3 2
♥ 7
♦ 9 8 7 5
♣ J 10 6

West	North	East	South
1♥	2♦	4♥	all pass

Contract 4♥ by West. North leads ♦K.

The count of winners is satisfactory: eight top tricks and two more available in spades. The count of losers is unsatisfactory: one possible spade loser and three possible club losers.

Of course, North MAY have ♠K and, by finessing twice, ten tricks could be made before clubs were played. Or, South MAY have ♣A, in which case there would be only two club losers.

However, these 'maybes' should be rejected when there is a totally safe alternative. After North's ♦K lead, he is certain to hold ♦Q (take this on trust if you must).

There is therefore a loser on loser play which will guarantee success. Take two rounds of trumps finishing in dummy. Lead ♦J and discard ♣6. North wins ♦Q but cannot, profitably, attack clubs. Magic *and* really easy!

Now you have time to establish two extra spade tricks without allowing the danger hand (South) to gain the lead and return a club. You cross to ♠A and play ♠Q discarding a club if South plays low.

Here South does have ♠K but it would not matter if North had it.

You would discard a club, North would win but the clubs are still protected.

A loser on loser play can also allow for swapping a dangerous, or impossible, ruff in one suit for a safer one in another.

♠ A K Q 4 2   ♠ 6 5 3
♥ A K 8 5   ♥ 7 6
♦ A   ♦ 8 7 6 5 4
♣ K 6 3   ♣ A 7 4

Contract 6♠ by West. North leads ♥Q.

The bidding was optimistic but the contract is not without hope. On the necessary assumption that the suits will divide with the odds, there are two heart losers and one club loser. What you would like to have been able to do is to ruff the two heart losers with East's two small trumps but this is obviously impossible since a defender will ruff the last heart with a higher trump.

The answer is to look to exchange one heart ruff for a club ruff. You cash ♥A K and ruff a heart. You play ♣A and ♣K and lead the fourth heart on which you discard East's last club (loser on loser). You should now be able to ruff the losing club.

Here is the complete deal:

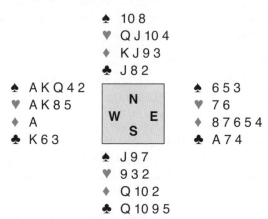

                   ♠ 10 8
                   ♥ Q J 10 4
                   ♦ K J 9 3
                   ♣ J 8 2

♠ A K Q 4 2   ♠ 6 5 3
♥ A K 8 5   ♥ 7 6
♦ A   ♦ 8 7 6 5 4
♣ K 6 3   ♣ A 7 4

                   ♠ J 9 7
                   ♥ 9 3 2
                   ♦ Q 10 2
                   ♣ Q 10 9 5

Following the proposed line of play, this would be the position with North on lead after six tricks had been played. A heart has been lost.

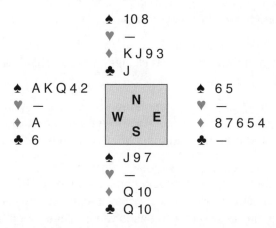

```
              ♠  10 8
              ♥  —
              ♦  K J 9 3
              ♣  J
♠ A K Q 4 2    ┌──────┐    ♠ 6 5
♥ —            │   N  │    ♥ —
♦ A            │ W  E │    ♦ 8 7 6 5 4
♣ 6            │   S  │    ♣ —
               └──────┘
              ♠  J 9 7
              ♥  —
              ♦  Q 10
              ♣  Q 10
```

Whatever North leads, he cannot prevent you ruffing ♣6 and winning the rest of the tricks.

quiz

Plan the play on this hand:

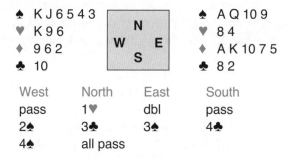

```
♠ K J 6 5 4 3   ┌──────┐   ♠ A Q 10 9
♥ K 9 6         │   N  │   ♥ 8 4
♦ 9 6 2         │ W  E │   ♦ A K 10 7 5
♣ 10            │   S  │   ♣ 8 2
                └──────┘
```

West	North	East	South
pass	1♥	dbl	pass
2♠	3♣	3♠	4♣
4♠	all pass		

Contract 4♠ by West. North leads ♣A followed by ♣K.

Count winners? Six spades and two diamonds.

Extra winners? Hearts: one can certainly be ruffed in the short (East) hand. Another, if South has ♥A, by leading towards ♥K 9 6. The bidding makes this very unlikely.

Diamonds: on an expected 3-2 split, the suit would provide two top winners and two more established winners. That looks much better.

Count losers? One club, one diamond and probably two hearts if North has ♥A. However ten tricks can be made if South can be prevented from gaining the lead. So there is a danger hand here.

Without sight of the North/South hands, a superficially attractive line of play is to draw trumps and play to establish two diamonds by hoping that it is North who has to win the third round. If South wins it, there is still that remote chance that he has ♥A. But the auction indicates that it is more likely that South has the longer diamonds since North has bid two suits.

There is a certain way to succeed if diamonds break 3-2. Instead of trumping ♣K at trick two, you should discard ♦2. This simply exchanges the diamond loser for an extra club loser but the gain is that you can ruff the third round of diamonds in your hand and East's two extra winners are established without losing the lead.

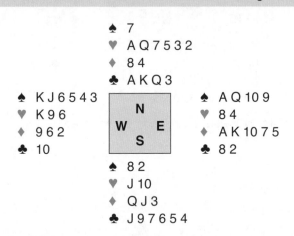

15 inferences

the bidding

As with a no trump contract, it is important to infer information from the auction. If an opponent has passed when he had a chance of opening the bidding, you can assume that he has less than twelve points. If he shows ten points during the play of the hand, you can safely place a missing queen with his partner.

For example:

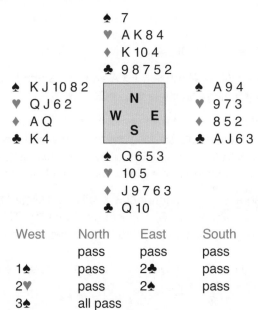

```
              ♠ 7
              ♥ A K 8 4
              ♦ K 10 4
              ♣ 9 8 7 5 2
♠ K J 10 8 2                    ♠ A 9 4
♥ Q J 6 2        N             ♥ 9 7 3
♦ A Q        W     E           ♦ 8 5 2
♣ K 4           S              ♣ A J 6 3
              ♠ Q 6 5 3
              ♥ 10 5
              ♦ J 9 7 6 3
              ♣ Q 10
```

West	North	East	South
	pass	pass	pass
1♠	pass	2♣	pass
2♥	pass	2♠	pass
3♠	all pass		

Contract 3♠ by West. North leads ♥A, ♥K and ♥4. South follows with ♥10, ♥5 and trumps the third round with ♠3. South then plays the ♦6. You try ♦Q, which loses to ♦K and North continues with ♥4.

North has shown ten points and cannot have either of the missing queens. This information shows you how to play the hand. You know that South has ♠Q. So you must trump ♥4 with ♠A in dummy. You then lead ♣9 to take the spade finesse through South.

If an opponent has opened with a suit bid at the one level, you can assume, unless there is some wild distribution around, that he has 12 or more points and at least four cards in the suit bid.

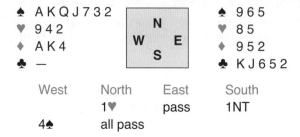

♠ AKQJ732			♠ 965
♥ 942			♥ 85
♦ AK4			♦ 952
♣ —			♣ KJ652

West	North	East	South
	1♥	pass	1NT
4♠	all pass		

Contract 4♠ by West. North leads ♥A and ♥K, South following with ♥7 and ♥6, and continues with ♥Q.

North's opening bid should alert you to the fact that he has not just the self-evident top hearts but long hearts as well and there is a danger that South can overruff East. If the third heart is to be trumped, then it must be with ♠9 in the hope that North has ♠10.

However, there is a much better play available. Discard a diamond from dummy on ♥Q – a loser on loser play. This will, almost certainly, allow a diamond to be trumped in dummy.

If an opponent opens 1NT, you can assume that he has a balanced hand with precisely 12–14 points.

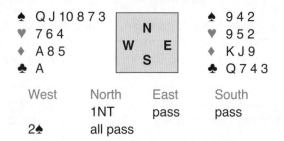

♠ QJ10873			♠ 942
♥ 764			♥ 952
♦ A85			♦ KJ9
♣ A			♣ Q743

West	North	East	South
	1NT	pass	pass
2♠	all pass		

Contract 2♠ by West. North leads ♥K which wins, ♥Q that also wins and ♥J, which is overtaken by South's ♥A. ♠6 is returned and North cashes ♠A, ♠K and exits with ♠5 (South discarding a diamond and a heart). We have reached this position and East is on lead:

♠ Q J 10		♠ —
♥ —	N	♥ —
♦ A 8 5	W E	♦ K J 9
♣ A	S	♣ Q 7 4 3

Count North's known points: ♥K Q J = 6; ♠A K = 7. Total = 13. The conclusion must be that South has ♦Q.

Five tricks have already been lost. How can you avoid a diamond loser, when the diamond finesse cannot win? South cannot be down to ♦Q x because it would be madness to have thrown a diamond away, as he did.

The lead is in dummy at the moment with ♣9. You must try a backward finesse in diamonds. This will work if North has ♦10. Lead ♦J. South must cover or ♦J will win. So you take ♦A and play towards ♦K 9, finessing if ♦10 does not appear.

This is the diamond layout that you are hoping for:

	♦ 10 x x	
♦ A 8 5		♦ K J 9
	♦ Q x x x	

Take note of the bidding and be aware that counting points can be as important as counting distribution.

the opening lead

A defender will not necessarily make the same lead against a suit contract as he would against a no trump contract. Against the latter he will often lead the fourth best of his longest suit because his objective is to establish small cards as winners. Obviously, this does not apply against a suit contract. The need is to establish defensive top winners rather than long suit winners. For example, against no trumps, and with South passing throughout, North would lead ♠3 from ♠K Q 7 3 2 but ♠K against a suit contract.

The lead of a small card, either as an opening lead or during the play, usually indicates that the leader has an honour card (A, K, Q, J or 10), plus at least two small ones behind it.

Aces, kings and queens are risky leads unless:

■ They are supported by the next honour (A K, K Q, Q J) or

■ They are doubleton and partner has bid that suit (A x, K x, Q x).

Note that with three cards in partner's suit, headed by an honour, the lowest is the normal lead. With three small cards, the middle one is the recommended choice with the higher one played the next time (Middle Up Down - known as MUD). This distinguishes an original holding of three small cards from a doubleton. Defenders have lead conventions to assist the defence but declarer can read the signals as well.

Here is just one example:

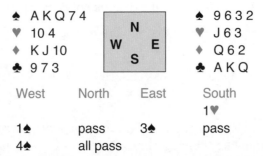

♠ A K Q 7 4		♠ 9 6 3 2
♥ 10 4	N	♥ J 6 3
♦ K J 10	W E	♦ Q 6 2
♣ 9 7 3	S	♣ A K Q

West	North	East	South
			1♥
1♠	pass	3♠	pass
4♠	all pass		

Contract 4♠ by West. North leads ♥5 and South wins ♥A, ♥K and continues with ♥Q. Should you trump this with a high spade (trumps will now have to divide 2-2) or a low spade? You cannot afford to lose a spade as you have already lost two hearts and must lose ♦A.

Have you been alert to the card played by North on the second round? If it was ♥2, then North has a doubleton and you must trump high and rely on the even trump split. If it was ♥7 or higher, then North started with three or four hearts and trumping small will suffice.

Declarer should always try to work out the significance of the opening lead. Why was it chosen?

the play

Did you notice how South followed on two of the earlier hands?

♠ K J 10 8 2		♠ A 9 4
♥ Q J 6 2	N	♥ 9 7 3
♦ A Q	W E	♦ 8 5 2
♣ K 4	S	♣ A J 6 3

Against West's 4♠ contract, North led ♥A K 4 and South followed with ♥10 5. There were other clues but the high-low play by South confirmed them. South was encouraging a continuation either because he had ♥Q (which you know is not the case) or he had a doubleton and was showing he could trump a third round of the suit.

It was exactly the same with:

♠ A K Q J 7 3 2		♠ 9 6 5
♥ 9 4 2	N	♥ 8 5
♦ A K 4	W E	♦ 9 5 2
♣ —	S	♣ K J 6 5 2

South followed with ♥7 and ♥6 when North led ♥A K, a confirmation that he held only two hearts.

If a defender makes an unexpected play, ask yourself why.

♠ Q 7 5 4 2		♠ K J
♥ Q 4 2	N	♥ K 9 7 5
♦ A K 8 6 4	W E	♦ Q 3
♣ —	S	♣ A 10 9 7 4

West	North	East	South
		1♣	pass
1♠	pass	2♣	pass
2♦	pass	2♠	all pass

Contract 2♠ by West. North leads ♠3.

South won the ♠A and switched to ♣K. Now this is an odd play. North's spade lead looks good, stopping dummy ruffing a loser. There is nowhere for you to discard club losers. Why didn't South play another trump?

When somebody plays an unexpected card always ask yourself why. Here the answer is clear – South hasn't got another trump! Which of course means that North must have five spades. You will need to make your small spades by ruffing since they will not become length winners. This is the full hand:

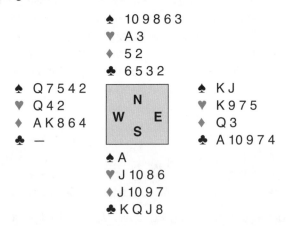

```
              ♠ 10 9 8 6 3
              ♥ A 3
              ♦ 5 2
              ♣ 6 5 3 2
♠ Q 7 5 4 2        N        ♠ K J
♥ Q 4 2                     ♥ K 9 7 5
♦ A K 8 6 4   W        E    ♦ Q 3
♣ —                S        ♣ A 10 9 7 4
              ♠ A
              ♥ J 10 8 6
              ♦ J 10 9 7
              ♣ K Q J 8
```

Win the ♣A and ruff a club. Cross back to dummy with ♦Q and lead another club to ruff. Try to cash your ♦A and ♦K. North can ruff the third diamond but you overruff with dummy's king and ruff another club.

You make the ♣A and three club ruffs, two diamonds, the ♠K as an overruff and the ♠Q in hand. Eight tricks made and maybe a ninth will come from a heart.

discovery

When an opponent who had the chance to open the bidding, but did not, cashes A K Q in a suit, he is showing you that he cannot have more than a queen outside. Defenders won't always help you by showing the high cards that they hold early in the play, thus assisting you in locating missing key cards.

Sometimes you can do some detective work.

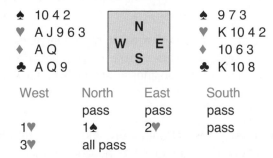

♠ 10 4 2		♠ 9 7 3
♥ A J 9 6 3		♥ K 10 4 2
♦ A Q		♦ 10 6 3
♣ A Q 9		♣ K 10 8

West	North	East	South
	pass	pass	pass
1♥	1♠	2♥	pass
3♥	all pass		

Contract 3♥ by West. North leads ♠A followed by ♠K (South plays ♠Q on this) and ♠J (on which South discards a small diamond). North gets off lead with a club. The problem is how to tackle trumps without losing a trick.

The best plan is to win the fourth trick with ♣K and take the diamond finesse. If it wins, you can afford to lose a trump trick. However, if it loses, you can confidently place South with ♥Q.

Count North's points: ♠A K J = 8; ♦K = 3; total = 11.

Holding the ♥Q, an extra two points, he would have opened the bidding rather than overcalled. You have 'discovered' that, since North holds ♦K, South holds ♥Q.

The same kind of play may dictate whether you can play the trump suit with the certainty of losing only one trick (a 'safety play') in it or need to take the chance of a favourable break.

```
♠ A K Q                    ♠ J 5 3
♥ 7 4 2          N         ♥ A K Q
♦ A K 9 4 3   W     E      ♦ J 5 2
♣ J 7            S         ♣ A Q 4 3
```

Contract 6♦ by West. North leads ♠10.

The problem, again, is how to tackle trumps. There is a certain way to avoid losing more than one diamond trick. It is to play ♦A and then ♦3 towards ♦J 5. Try it out to make sure that it always works.

But . . . you cannot afford the luxury of this safety play if you are going to lose a club trick. Therefore, what you must do is to find out. You should take the club finesse at trick two. If it wins, you can afford to play trumps in the safe way to ensure you make the contract.

If the club finesse loses to South's ♣K, you have to play off ♦A K and hope that one defender holds a doubleton ♦Q x.

watch the discards

There's trouble enough trying to count points and distribution but you should try to watch what a defender discards when unable to follow suit. Usually, he will discard something he can afford but even that can be a source of information.

Sometimes . . . he will try to help his partner by discarding an unusually high card in another suit which indicates that he would like it led if his partner gets the lead.

Sometimes . . . he will discard a low card indicating that he does not want that suit led.

Every little helps!

16 let the defence assist

There was a hand earlier in this book when a defender was put on lead and obliged to open up a suit in which declarer held Q x x opposite J x x in dummy. This enabled declarer to win a trick in the suit that would not be available if he had to lead it himself.

On this hand the defence is forced to give declarer a trick:

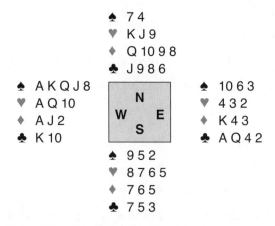

♠ 7 4
♥ K J 9
♦ Q 10 9 8
♣ J 9 8 6

♠ A K Q J 8
♥ A Q 10
♦ A J 2
♣ K 10

♠ 10 6 3
♥ 4 3 2
♦ K 4 3
♣ A Q 4 2

♠ 9 5 2
♥ 8 7 6 5
♦ 7 6 5
♣ 7 5 3

Contract 6♠ by West. North leads ♣4.

You are assured of eleven tricks (five spades, one heart, two diamonds and three clubs). After you have drawn trumps, ending in dummy with ♠10, there are finesses available in all three of the other suits. It is a confusing choice, which ones to try.

There is, however, a certain way to make the contract without relying on a favourable distribution. You play a heart at trick four and cover whatever card South plays. Here, you would play ♥10 when South plays low. If North wins with the ♥J, he has to give away the twelfth trick in whichever suit he chooses since you hold a tenace in all three. A tenace is a broken suit holding like A Q 10.

The technique of losing a trick at a critical point that forces a defender to make a lead to your advantage is called an endplay. An endplay can occur in a no trump contract as well as in a suit contract.

endplays with trumps

There is great advantage about having a trump suit in the matter of engineering an endplay. We have, briefly, met it before – the ruff and discard.

To take advantage of this type of endplay, the following conditions need to apply:

- Trumps have been drawn.

- Declarer and dummy have at least one outstanding trump each.

- The defender put on lead has no safe exit card.

```
  ♠ A K Q 7        ┌─────────┐      ♠ 8 6 3 2
  ♥ A J 5          │    N    │      ♥ K 10 6
  ♦ A 3            │ W     E │      ♦ 10 7
  ♣ K J 7 3        │    S    │      ♣ A Q 9 2
                   └─────────┘
```

Contract 6♠ by West. North leads ♦K.

The balanced distribution means that there are only eleven sure tricks. It may seem that the extra one needs an inspired view about the position of ♥Q but, provided trumps split 3-2, the contract is certain.

You win ♦A, draw trumps, cash all four club winners and exit with a diamond.

It matters not whether North or South wins this trick. Whoever does simply has a choice of which way he surrenders.

Either . . . he leads a heart and the guess in hearts is removed.

Or . . . he leads a diamond allowing a heart to be discarded from one hand and ruffed in the other (the ruff and discard). It doesn't matter which hand does what.

This is a certain endplay. Club winners were taken after trumps were drawn to remove any chance of a defender getting off lead in that suit. This is called an elimination.

West		East
♠ K Q J 10		♠ 8 6 3 2
♥ A J 5	N	♥ K 10 9
♦ A 3	W E	♦ 4 2
♣ K 8 7 3	S	♣ A 5 4 2

Contract 4♠ by West. North leads ♦Q.

A spade, a diamond and a club are inevitable losers. You do not want to lose a heart as well. The good thing is that neither defender can lead a heart without solving the problem of which way to finesse in that suit.

You should win the first trick and drive out ♠A. Whoever holds ♠A will not be able to lead a heart. Say a diamond is cashed, another spade is led to which the other defender follows. The last trump is drawn and ♣A K and another club is played. Unless clubs break 4-1, whichever defender wins the third round is endplayed having to lead a heart or give a ruff and discard by leading a diamond.

Try to put your opponent in a position where he has to help you

partial elimination

The perfect endplay arrives when you know that the defender has no card that he can safely lead. They have been eliminated in the preparation.

Sometimes, you have to HOPE that the hand you are endplaying has run out of cards in a particular suit.

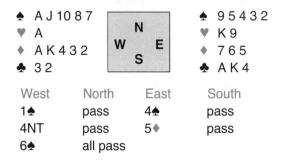

	♠ A J 10 8 7			♠ 9 5 4 3 2
♥ A				♥ K 9
♦ A K 4 3 2				♦ 7 6 5
♣ 3 2				♣ A K 4

West	North	East	South
1♠	pass	4♠	pass
4NT	pass	5♦	pass
6♠	all pass		

Contract 6♠ by West. North leads ♣Q.

You have been adventurous in the bidding but maybe the gods will be kind.

There is an inevitable trump loser and another in diamonds. However, there is the possibility of an endplay to avoid the diamond loser. It needs trumps to break 2-1 and needs the defender who wins the second round of trumps to have started with only two diamonds.

You win the first trick, cash ♠A and then eliminate hearts and clubs. You cash ♥A, cross to dummy with ♣A, cash the ♥K throwing a diamond, cash ♣K and ruff a club in hand. Then you cash ♦A K and play a second trump. If the defender who wins the spade has only hearts and clubs left, he will have to give away a ruff and discard. You ruff in your hand and discard the diamond from East's hand.

This is known as a partial elimination. Partial because it is not certain that all the exit cards have been removed from the hand that is thrown in.

17 a really easy squeeze

What is a squeeze?

It is simply a descriptive term for the situation where one defender – sometimes both – is under pressure and has to discard in a suit that he wants to guard. Consequently, declarer is able to make an extra trick in the suit that has been unguarded.

Squeezes are generally put into the category of advanced play. The general consensus is that they should not even be mentioned in the company of those starting their bridge careers. In truth, many squeezes happen by accident rather than design. There is an easily understood technique, which can help you make what seem like impossible contracts.

♠ A 10 2		♠ 9 5 4
♥ A K 7 4 3		♥ Q J 8
♦ 10 3		♦ A K Q 2
♣ A K 4		♣ 9 7 3

Contract 6♥ by West. North leads ♠K.

There are eleven top winners, assuming trumps break no worse than 4-1, but not a sniff of the necessary twelfth.

There is a chance, however, if the first trick is ducked. The technical term for this is rectifying the count. It means that, when you need one extra trick, and can see no legitimate way of making it, you lose the tricks that you can afford to lose and then take your winning tricks.

Here, the way to lose a trick you can afford to lose is to refuse to win the first trick.

Look at what may result, if you are lucky:

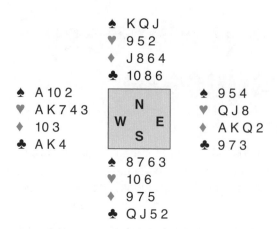

No doubt, ♠Q will follow at trick two and ♠A must be taken. See what happens when you now cash four rounds of trumps. You discard ♠9 from dummy on the fourth trump and are about to play the fifth heart.

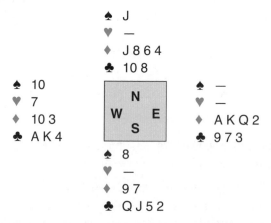

For the moment, North has a safe club discard of the ♣8. The ♣3 is thrown from dummy but, when you cash ♣A K, North is squeezed. If he discards the ♠J, your ♠10 becomes a winner. If he discards the ♦4, East's ♦2 becomes a winner.

The hand virtually plays itself if you simply arrange to lose the one trick that you can safely afford early in the play.

hands to play and practise

The primary objective in learning bridge is to get four people round a table playing the game and enjoying the stimulating challenge that it presents – the sooner the better. The thirty hands that follow are based on the techniques explained in this book. While they can be studied from the text, it will be more instructive and much greater fun, if you have two or three friends who can play them with you. Since one person is always dummy, you can play perfectly satisfactorily with three players by having the missing one sitting East (the dummy).

Prepare the hands in advance from the complete deal given with the answers. Sort the pack into suits and distribute the suit as shown. Store the complete deal in four envelopes marked W, N, E or S with the hand number on it. Note North's opening lead and any other instructions.

Six deals will normally be enough to play in one session since you will want time for discussion. The person who prepared a particular deal should not be the declarer when it is played. Make that player East if there are four players, or a defender if only three. Give everyone a go at being declarer (West).

During the play, everybody (including dummy) plays a card in turn. They put the card down directly in front of themselves. When the four cards to a trick have been played, each card is turned face down, upright when a player's side has won the trick and lengthways when it has been lost.

In the diagram on the next page West (the declarer) has won the first three tricks but lost the fourth.

After the play, you count the number of cards pointing in your direction to work out the number of tricks won by your side. Each player's original hand has been retained and the deal can be

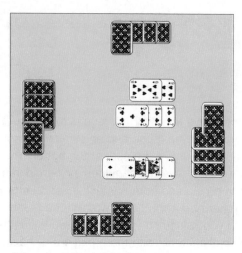

revised with all four hands visible. You can even play the hand
again with a different declarer to check that the lesson is
understood.

There is no magic formula for declarer play. If there were, bridge
would never be the lifetime's challenge that is its great attraction.

This book is intended only to set you on the way and map out the
attractions that lie ahead. One thing is certain. You will derive the
greatest benefit and stimulation from the game only if you are
prepared to give some thought to it. If you have a sleepless night
wondering whether you should have made that contract, the
omens are good.

The first fifteen hands are intended to be easier than the next
fifteen. On all of them it is far more important to understand how
the contract should be played than it is to get it right first time.
Bridge is primarily for fun. Its attraction is the intellectual
challenge that it offers and the satisfaction gained, at all levels of
ability, in logically working out the right line of play. In this respect,
much comes with practice and experience.

In all the problems you are declarer (West) and your task is to
plan the play.

hands to play

1

♠ 9 8		♠ 7 6 5
♥ A K	N	♥ J 9 8
♦ Q 10 9 8 5	W E	♦ A K J 4 2
♣ A K 4 2	S	♣ 6 5

West	North	East	South
1♦	pass	3♦	pass
5♦	all pass		

Contract 5♦ by West. North leads ♣J.

2

♠ K Q 6 5 4		♠ A 10 2
♥ A K 2	N	♥ 9 6 4
♦ Q 6	W E	♦ K J 10 9
♣ A 4 3	S	♣ 10 6 5

West	North	East	South
1♠	pass	1NT	pass
2NT	pass	3♠	pass
4♠	all pass		

Contract 4♠ by West. North leads ♣K.

3

♠ A K Q J 5		♠ 10 2
♥ 2	N	♥ Q J 9 8 3
♦ A Q 8 6 4	W E	♦ K 2
♣ 3 2	S	♣ K 7 6 4

West	North	East	South
1♠	pass	2♥	pass
3♦	pass	3♠	pass
4♠	all pass		

Contract 4♠ by West. North leads ♣Q.

1

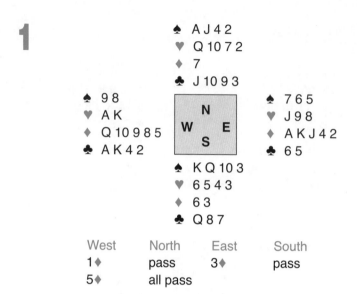

♠ A J 4 2
♥ Q 10 7 2
♦ 7
♣ J 10 9 3

♠ 9 8
♥ A K
♦ Q 10 9 8 5
♣ A K 4 2

♠ 7 6 5
♥ J 9 8
♦ A K J 4 2
♣ 6 5

♠ K Q 10 3
♥ 6 5 4 3
♦ 6 3
♣ Q 8 7

West	North	East	South
1♦	pass	3♦	pass
5♦	all pass		

Contract 5♦ by West. North leads ♣J.

Declarer should do his counting, look for problems . . . and find none!

He should win the first trick and draw trumps. Even if they divide 3-0 there are adequate resources and entries to ruff two club losers.

Yes . . . there are many hands which do, virtually, play themselves.

2

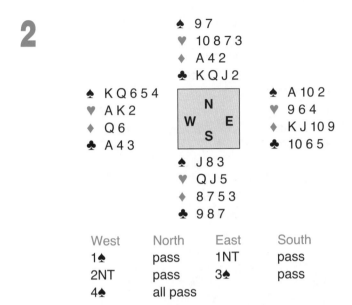

♠ 9 7
♥ 10 8 7 3
♦ A 4 2
♣ K Q J 2

♠ K Q 6 5 4
♥ A K 2
♦ Q 6
♣ A 4 3

N
W   E
S

♠ A 10 2
♥ 9 6 4
♦ K J 10 9
♣ 10 6 5

♠ J 8 3
♥ Q J 5
♦ 8 7 5 3
♣ 9 8 7

West	North	East	South
1♠	pass	1NT	pass
2NT	pass	3♠	pass
4♠	all pass		

Contract 4♠ by West. North leads ♣K.

There are four losers to be counted (one heart, one diamond and two clubs) but one of them, ♥2, can be discarded on a master diamond in East's hand once ♦A has been driven out. The count of winners, including the established diamonds, is satisfactory.

However there is a slight problem.

If trumps are drawn in three rounds before diamonds are played, West would then lead ♦Q but North could refuse to win ♦A and take it on the second round of the suit.

He would cash his two winning clubs and exit with a heart. There would be master diamonds in dummy but no entry to make them.

Therefore, declarer must cash just ♠K and ♠Q before driving out ♦A and, when he gets the lead, ♠A will provide the required entry to dummy while drawing the last trump.

3

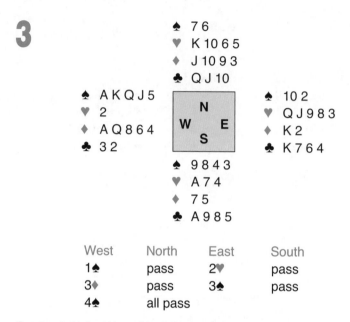

	♠ 7 6	
	♥ K 10 6 5	
	♦ J 10 9 3	
	♣ Q J 10	

♠ A K Q J 5	N	♠ 10 2
♥ 2	W E	♥ Q J 9 8 3
♦ A Q 8 6 4	S	♦ K 2
♣ 3 2		♣ K 7 6 4

	♠ 9 8 4 3	
	♥ A 7 4	
	♦ 7 5	
	♣ A 9 8 5	

West	North	East	South
1♠	pass	2♥	pass
3♦	pass	3♠	pass
4♠	all pass		

Contract 4♠ by West. North leads ♣Q.

There is no point in playing ♣K from dummy, North won't have ♣A Q J but South's ♣A might just be with only one or two small cards. Not so in this case and West ruffs the third round of clubs.

West can count five spades and three diamond winners. If the diamonds break 3-3 there will be five diamond tricks, but a 4-2 break is more likely. West can ruff a diamond in dummy but must do this before drawing trumps.

West plays a diamond to the king, back to the diamond ace and a small diamond, ruffing with the TEN of spades. Ruffing with a low spade is not good enough.

Now dummy's low trump is led and West draws four rounds of trumps before cashing the winning diamonds.

hands to play

4

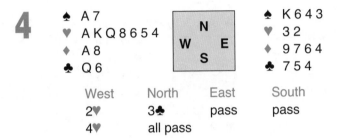

♠ A 7			♠ K 6 4 3
♥ A K Q 8 6 5 4			♥ 3 2
♦ A 8			♦ 9 7 6 4
♣ Q 6			♣ 7 5 4

West	North	East	South
2♥	3♣	pass	pass
4♥	all pass		

Contract 4♥ by West. North leads ♣A then ♣K and then ♣2. South follows with ♣9, ♣3 and ruffs the third club with ♥9.

5

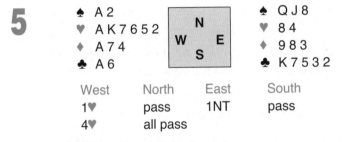

♠ A 2			♠ Q J 8
♥ A K 7 6 5 2			♥ 8 4
♦ A 7 4			♦ 9 8 3
♣ A 6			♣ K 7 5 3 2

West	North	East	South
1♥	pass	1NT	pass
4♥	all pass		

Contract 4♥ by West. North leads ♣Q.

6

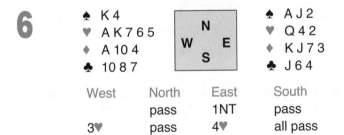

♠ K 4			♠ A J 2
♥ A K 7 6 5			♥ Q 4 2
♦ A 10 4			♦ K J 7 3
♣ 10 8 7			♣ J 6 4

West	North	East	South
	pass	1NT	pass
3♥	pass	4♥	all pass

Contract 4♥ by West. North leads ♣ A K Q and exits with ♥J.

4

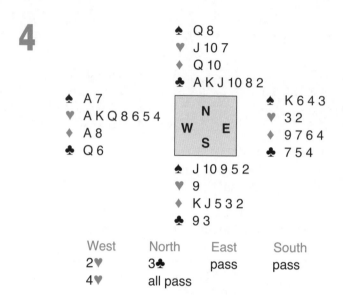

```
              ♠ Q 8
              ♥ J 10 7
              ♦ Q 10
              ♣ A K J 10 8 2
♠ A 7                              ♠ K 6 4 3
♥ A K Q 8 6 5 4        N          ♥ 3 2
♦ A 8           W         E       ♦ 9 7 6 4
♣ Q 6                  S          ♣ 7 5 4
              ♠ J 10 9 5 2
              ♥ 9
              ♦ K J 5 3 2
              ♣ 9 3
```

West	North	East	South
2♥	3♣	pass	pass
4♥	all pass		

Contract 4♥ by West. North leads ♣A then ♣K and then ♣2.
South follows with ♣9, ♣3 and ruffs the third club with ♥9.

West made a good bid when he jumped to 4♥. Now he must
make sure he plays as well as he bids.

Suppose he carelessly overruffs South's ♥9 and North turns up
with ♥J 10 7? A trump trick will now have to be lost in addition to
the two clubs and a diamond loser.

Instead of overtrumping, West should simply discard that
'inescapable' losing diamond. Now ten tricks can be made without
a problem.

Note North's ♣2 on the third round which forces South to ruff and
makes it possible for North's ♥J 10 7 to be promoted into a trump
trick.

5

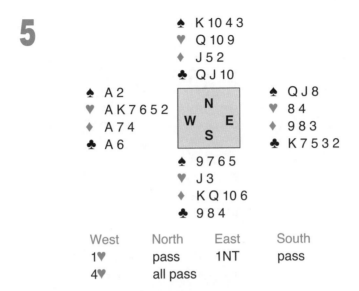

```
              ♠ K 10 4 3
              ♥ Q 10 9
              ♦ J 5 2
              ♣ Q J 10
  ♠ A 2                        ♠ Q J 8
  ♥ A K 7 6 5 2      N         ♥ 8 4
  ♦ A 7 4        W     E       ♦ 9 8 3
  ♣ A 6              S         ♣ K 7 5 3 2
              ♠ 9 7 6 5
              ♥ J 3
              ♦ K Q 10 6
              ♣ 9 8 4
```

West	North	East	South
1♥	pass	1NT	pass
4♥	all pass		

Contract 4♥ by West. North leads ♣Q.

There are four possible losers (one spade, one heart and two diamonds): one too many. Lack of sufficient entries to dummy means that East's long clubs cannot provide extra tricks.

However, East's ♠Q J can provide both an extra winner and an opportunity to discard a diamond loser.

A spade loser would be avoided, if South holds ♠K. But, to take the finesse means using dummy's only entry, ♣K. If the finesse loses, a spade winner is stranded in dummy.

Declarer should win the first trick in hand, play ♥A K and then ♠A 2, establishing a spade winner. ♣K will be the entry to cash ♠Q (or ♠J) and discard a diamond loser.

6

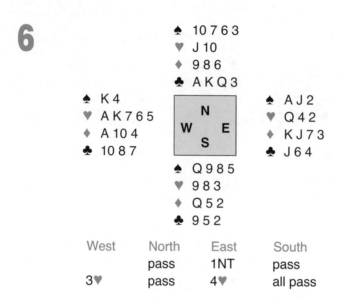

```
                    ♠ 10 7 6 3
                    ♥ J 10
                    ♦ 9 8 6
                    ♣ A K Q 3
  ♠ K 4                              ♠ A J 2
  ♥ A K 7 6 5          N            ♥ Q 4 2
  ♦ A 10 4        W        E        ♦ K J 7 3
  ♣ 10 8 7            S             ♣ J 6 4
                    ♠ Q 9 8 5
                    ♥ 9 8 3
                    ♦ Q 5 2
                    ♣ 9 5 2
```

West	North	East	South
	pass	1NT	pass
3♥	pass	4♥	all pass

Contract 4♥ by West. North leads ♣A K Q and exits with ♥J.

With three tricks already lost, declarer must win the remainder.

North has helped to solve this problem by revealing ten points on the first four tricks. With ♠Q or ♦Q, he would have twelve points and is highly likely to have opened the bidding. Both those queens can be assumed to be in South's hand.

Declarer should disregard the spade finesse and, after drawing trumps, should play for South to hold ♦Q to make his tenth trick.

After drawing trumps, ending in West's hand, a small diamond should be led. If North does not produce ♦Q (he might have decided not to open with 12 points and ♦Q singleton), East's ♦K is played and the diamond finesse taken through South.

hands to play

7

♠ K 9 2		♠ A 4 3
♥ K Q 7 6 5	N	♥ J 10 4 2
♦ K 6	W E	♦ Q J 8
♣ A 5 4	S	♣ Q 7 6

West	North	East	South
1♥	pass	3♥	pass
4♥	all pass		

Contract 4♥ by West. North leads ♠Q.

8

♠ A 9 7		♠ Q J 10
♥ A 4 3	N	♥ 9 7 5
♦ A K Q J 9 7	W E	♦ 6 5 4 3
♣ 2	S	♣ A 7 4

West	North	East	South
2♦	3♣	5♦	all pass

Contract 5♦ by West. North leads ♣K.

9

♠ A J 6 4 2		♠ 3
♥ A 7 5 3 2	N	♥ 9 8 6 4
♦ K 7	W E	♦ A J 4 3
♣ 2	S	♣ A Q 6 4

West	North	East	South
1♠	pass	2♣	pass
2♥	pass	4♥	all pass

Contract 4♥ by West. North leads ♥K.

7

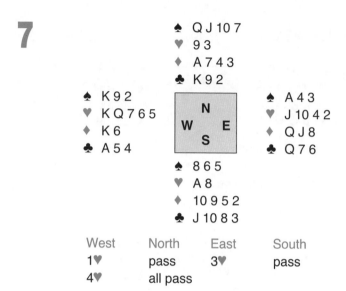

♠ Q J 10 7
♥ 9 3
♦ A 7 4 3
♣ K 9 2

♠ K 9 2
♥ K Q 7 6 5
♦ K 6
♣ A 5 4

♠ A 4 3
♥ J 10 4 2
♦ Q J 8
♣ Q 7 6

♠ 8 6 5
♥ A 8
♦ 10 9 5 2
♣ J 10 8 3

West	North	East	South
1♥	pass	3♥	pass
4♥	all pass		

Contract 4♥ by West. North leads ♠Q.

There is a potential loser in spades, a certain one in both hearts and diamonds and . . . one or two in clubs.

There is a way of getting rid of a spade loser by winning the first trick with ♠K and playing ♦K followed, if ♦A is not taken, by ♦6. ♠A is a sure entry to the established diamond winner.

Therefore driving out ♦A must take priority over driving out ♥A.

With one loser eliminated, declarer must hope that another will be avoided – and an extra winner materialises – by playing towards East's ♣Q. This is just a 50% chance but, when North holds ♣K, the contract makes.

8

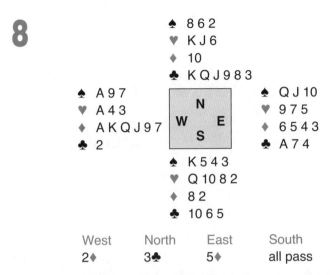

```
                    ♠ 8 6 2
                    ♥ K J 6
                    ♦ 10
                    ♣ K Q J 9 8 3
♠ A 9 7                              ♠ Q J 10
♥ A 4 3           N                  ♥ 9 7 5
♦ A K Q J 9 7   W     E              ♦ 6 5 4 3
♣ 2               S                  ♣ A 7 4
                    ♠ K 5 4 3
                    ♥ Q 10 8 2
                    ♦ 8 2
                    ♣ 10 6 5
```

West	North	East	South
2♦	3♣	5♦	all pass

Contract 5♦ by West. North leads ♣K.

Since West was showing at least eight playing tricks, maybe East, who can provide the ninth, should have bid 3NT. If West thinks this way, there is the danger that he may be distracted from the problem in hand which is that, after winning ♣A, he has to take ten more tricks.

Like it or not, West has to assume that, despite North's overcall, South has ♠K and that North has to follow suit to two rounds. The spade finesse must be taken at trick two and repeated if South does not cover.

As it happens, all is well and both East and West should rest content. Even in matchpointed pairs 5♦ will score equally with 3NT. Taking the spade finesse in the latter contract would be evidence of a deathwish.

9

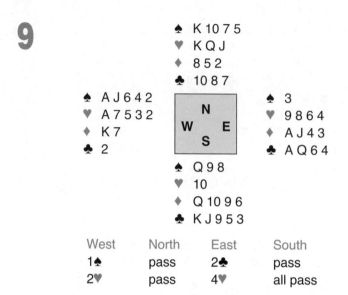

♠ K 10 7 5
♥ K Q J
♦ 8 5 2
♣ 10 8 7

♠ A J 6 4 2
♥ A 7 5 3 2
♦ K 7
♣ 2

N
W   E
S

♠ 3
♥ 9 8 6 4
♦ A J 4 3
♣ A Q 6 4

♠ Q 9 8
♥ 10
♦ Q 10 9 6
♣ K J 9 5 3

West	North	East	South
1♠	pass	2♣	pass
2♥	pass	4♥	all pass

Contract 4♥ by West. North leads ♥K.

The count of winners in the side suits shows one spade, two diamonds and one club. You could draw trumps, but if they break 3-1, which is likely on the lead, you will make only three trump tricks plus a ruff in the East hand. With both the club and diamond finesses wrong you will go down.

When the trump suit holding is poor it is better to try to win your trumps separately if you can, and with a singleton in each hand you can cross-ruff your way to success.

You should win ♥K lead with ♥A. Do not draw the remaining trumps. Cash ♦K and ♦A and ruff a diamond. Cash ♠A and ruff a spade, cash ♣A and ruff a club, ruff a spade, ruff a club and ruff a spade. You have now won eleven tricks. The only tricks for the defence are ♥Q and ♥J.

When you embark on a cross-ruff it is best to cash your side suit winners first (in this case diamonds) otherwise a defender may be able to throw away and trump your winners at the end.

hands to play

10

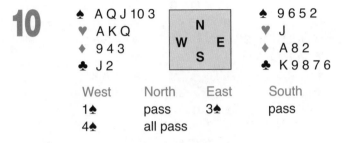

♠ A Q J 10 3
♥ A K Q
♦ 9 4 3
♣ J 2

♠ 9 6 5 2
♥ J
♦ A 8 2
♣ K 9 8 7 6

West	North	East	South
1♠	pass	3♠	pass
4♠	all pass		

Contract 4♠ by West. North leads ♦K.

11

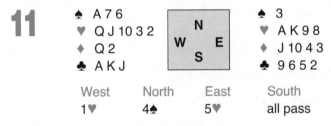

♠ A 7 6
♥ Q J 10 3 2
♦ Q 2
♣ A K J

♠ 3
♥ A K 9 8
♦ J 10 4 3
♣ 9 6 5 2

West	North	East	South
1♥	4♠	5♥	all pass

Contract 5♥ by West. North leads ♠K.

If declarer leads a heart at trick two, North shows out.

12

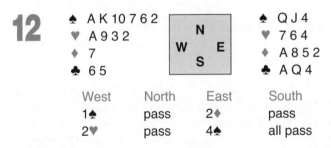

♠ A K 10 7 6 2
♥ A 9 3 2
♦ 7
♣ 6 5

♠ Q J 4
♥ 7 6 4
♦ A 8 5 2
♣ A Q 4

West	North	East	South
1♠	pass	2♦	pass
2♥	pass	4♠	all pass

Contract 4♠ by West. North leads ♦K.

10

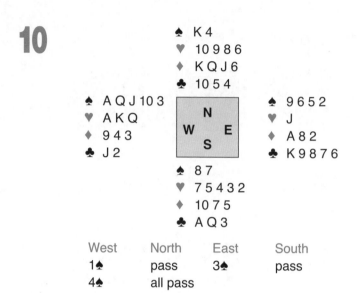

	♠ K 4	
	♥ 10 9 8 6	
	♦ K Q J 6	
	♣ 10 5 4	
♠ A Q J 10 3		♠ 9 6 5 2
♥ A K Q	N	♥ J
♦ 9 4 3	W E	♦ A 8 2
♣ J 2	S	♣ K 9 8 7 6
	♠ 8 7	
	♥ 7 5 4 3 2	
	♦ 10 7 5	
	♣ A Q 3	

West	North	East	South
1♠	pass	3♠	pass
4♠	all pass		

Contract 4♠ by West. North leads ♦K.

Declarer should count five possible losers: one spade, two diamonds and two clubs.

On a good day, South would have ♠K and North would have ♣A. Taking the spade finesse and playing towards East's ♣K would work.

There is, however, no need to risk either of these plays. Two losing diamonds in East's hand can be discarded on the top hearts in West's hand.

Declarer should win ♦A and cash ♥A K Q immediately, discarding East's ♦8 2. He then trumps a diamond with a small spade and returns to his hand with ♠A and trumps his last diamond with ♠9. If that happens to get overtrumped it can only be with ♠K which declarer is prepared to lose anyway.

11

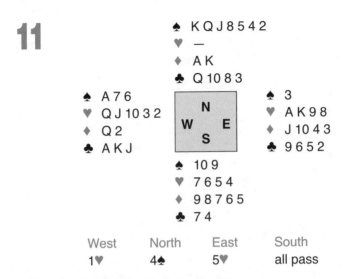

```
                    ♠ K Q J 8 5 4 2
                    ♥ —
                    ♦ A K
                    ♣ Q 10 8 3
♠ A 7 6                                  ♠ 3
♥ Q J 10 3 2        N                    ♥ A K 9 8
♦ Q 2           W       E                ♦ J 10 4 3
♣ A K J             S                    ♣ 9 6 5 2
                    ♠ 10 9
                    ♥ 7 6 5 4
                    ♦ 9 8 7 6 5
                    ♣ 7 4
```

West	North	East	South
1♥	4♠	5♥	all pass

Contract 5♥ by West. North leads ♠K.

♠A and two spade ruffs in dummy will produce three tricks and West can add five trump winners and two top clubs. That would be the best way of playing the hand if the contract had been 4♥.

However, eleven tricks must be made in 5♥. That means that, in addition to ruffing two spades, either a diamond winner needs to be established in East's hand or ♣J must make a trick. The diamond winner is the better alternative but a trump entry will need to be retained in dummy.

Declarer might cash ♥Q first but, after discovering that South has four trumps, should switch to ♦Q. North will play another spade, dummy ruffs with ♥A or ♥K and ♦J forces out the second master diamond. Another spade from North can be ruffed with the second top trump; ♦10 cashed to discard ♣J and declarer can then draw trumps and has eleven tricks.

Playing on diamonds at trick two works as well.

12

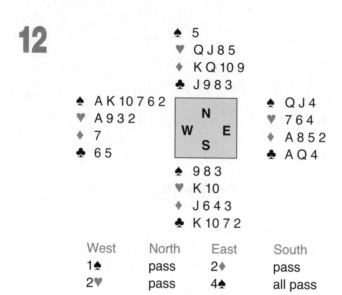

♠ 5
♥ Q J 8 5
♦ K Q 10 9
♣ J 9 8 3

♠ A K 10 7 6 2
♥ A 9 3 2
♦ 7
♣ 6 5

♠ Q J 4
♥ 7 6 4
♦ A 8 5 2
♣ A Q 4

♠ 9 8 3
♥ K 10
♦ J 6 4 3
♣ K 10 7 2

West	North	East	South
1♠	pass	2♦	pass
2♥	pass	4♠	all pass

Contract 4♠ by West. North leads ♦K.

A count of losers after trumps have been drawn in three rounds leaves three hearts and one club. Declarer would then have to hope that hearts divided 3-3 or that North held ♣K and a winning finesse could be taken.

It is much better to arrange to trump a possible heart loser in dummy.

West can win ♦A and play a heart to ♥A and another heart. He has time to play another heart when he regains the lead and, subsequently, he will be able to trump his fourth heart with East's ♠Q or ♠J and make his tenth trick in so doing.

hands to play

13

♠ J 10 6 4 2			♠ A K Q
♥ 4 3 2			♥ Q 8 7
♦ A 6 4	N W E S		♦ 3 2
♣ A K			♣ Q J 10 6 5

West	North	East	South
		1NT	pass
3♠	pass	4♠	all pass

Contract 4♠ by West. North leads ♥J.

14

♠ A K Q			♠ 8 7 2
♥ A K J 10 4 2			♥ Q 9 3
♦ 3	N W E S		♦ K 6 5 4
♣ A K J			♣ 9 7 6

West	North	East	South
2♣	pass	2♦	pass
2♥	pass	3♥	pass
6♥	all pass		

Contract 6♥ by West. North leads ♠J.

15

♠ Q J 10 9 8			♠ K 6 2
♥ A K 6 4			♥ J 7
♦ K 7 6	N W E S		♦ 5 3 2
♣ 4			♣ A 9 8 3 2

West	North	East	South
1♠	pass	1NT	pass
2♥	pass	3♠	pass
4♠	all pass		

Contract 4♠ by West. North leads ♦Q.

13

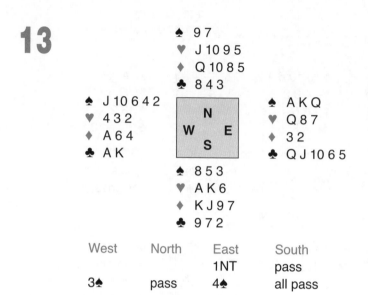

♠ J 10 6 4 2   ♠ A K Q
♥ 4 3 2   ♥ Q 8 7
♦ A 6 4   ♦ 3 2
♣ A K   ♣ Q J 10 6 5

♠ 8 5 3
♥ A K 6
♦ K J 9 7
♣ 9 7 2

West	North	East	South
		1NT	pass
3♠	pass	4♠	all pass

Contract 4♠ by West. North leads ♥J.

After losing three hearts, West has eleven winners – five spades, one diamond and five clubs! It seems more than enough. The only problem is that if West draws the opponents' trumps and cashes ♣A and ♣K, there is no entry back to dummy to cash the remaining clubs.

The solution is to cash just two top trumps, then cash the two top clubs. Now ♠Q is the entry to dummy, which both draws the trumps and provides an entry to the three remaining club winners.

Note that West was quite correct to bid 3♠ on an unexciting suit.

14

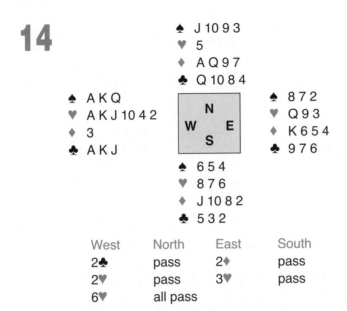

	♠ J 10 9 3	
	♥ 5	
	♦ A Q 9 7	
	♣ Q 10 8 4	
♠ A K Q		♠ 8 7 2
♥ A K J 10 4 2	N	♥ Q 9 3
♦ 3	W E	♦ K 6 5 4
♣ A K J	S	♣ 9 7 6
	♠ 6 5 4	
	♥ 8 7 6	
	♦ J 10 8 2	
	♣ 5 3 2	

West	North	East	South
2♣	pass	2♦	pass
2♥	pass	3♥	pass
6♥	all pass		

Contract 6♥ by West. North leads ♣J.

Declarer has two chances of success: either North holds ♦A or South holds ♣Q.

If trumps are drawn in three rounds ending in dummy, the contract will depend on on the club finesse alone. West must play just two top trumps, keeping an entry in East's hand and then play ♦3 towards dummy.

Had South held ♦A, the club finesse could still be taken.

15

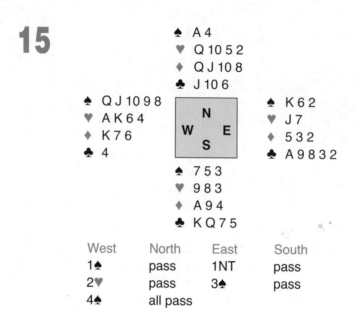

```
                    ♠ A 4
                    ♥ Q 10 5 2
                    ♦ Q J 10 8
                    ♣ J 10 6
  ♠ Q J 10 9 8              ♠ K 6 2
  ♥ A K 6 4         N       ♥ J 7
  ♦ K 7 6      W       E    ♦ 5 3 2
  ♣ 4              S        ♣ A 9 8 3 2
                    ♠ 7 5 3
                    ♥ 9 8 3
                    ♦ A 9 4
                    ♣ K Q 7 5
```

West	North	East	South
1♠	pass	1NT	pass
2♥	pass	3♠	pass
4♠	all pass		

Contract 4♠ by West. North leads ♦Q.

Somewhat optimistic bidding gets East/West to 4♠. North's ♦Q lead solves one problem for West since there are now only two diamond losers. South wins ♦A and returns ♦9. However there are also one spade and two heart losers to worry about.

The winners are four spades (after the ace has gone) two hearts, a diamond and a club. The extra tricks will have to come from ruffing the two losing hearts in dummy. The only other possibility is to set up the long clubs but the East hand does not have enough entries to do this.

West wins ♦K and cashes ♥A and ♥K. A low heart is ruffed with East's ♠6. Even if South started with only two hearts, using the six may stop an overruff. ♣A is cashed and a club is ruffed. Now West plays the last heart and ruffs in dummy with ♠K. That way there is no danger of an overruff.

Remember the tip 'Always ruff with the highest trump you can spare'.

hands to play

16

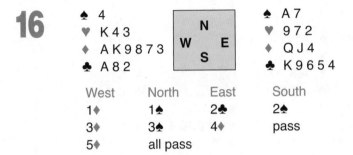

♠	4
♥	K 4 3
♦	A K 9 8 7 3
♣	A 8 2

♠	A 7
♥	9 7 2
♦	Q J 4
♣	K 9 6 5 4

West	North	East	South
1♦	1♠	2♣	2♠
3♦	3♠	4♦	pass
5♦	all pass		

Contract 5♦ by West. North leads ♠K.

17

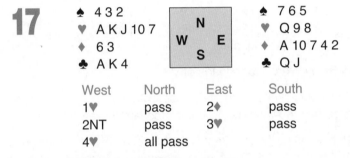

♠	4 3 2
♥	A K J 10 7
♦	6 3
♣	A K 4

♠	7 6 5
♥	Q 9 8
♦	A 10 7 4 2
♣	Q J

West	North	East	South
1♥	pass	2♦	pass
2NT	pass	3♥	pass
4♥	all pass		

Contract 4♥ by West. North leads ♦K.

18

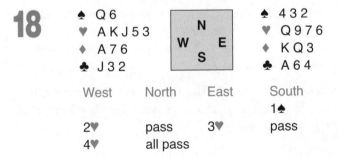

♠	Q 6
♥	A K J 5 3
♦	A 7 6
♣	J 3 2

♠	4 3 2
♥	Q 9 7 6
♦	K Q 3
♣	A 6 4

West	North	East	South
			1♠
2♥	pass	3♥	pass
4♥	all pass		

Contract 4♥ by West. North leads ♠J. South cashes ♠A K and plays ♠5.

16

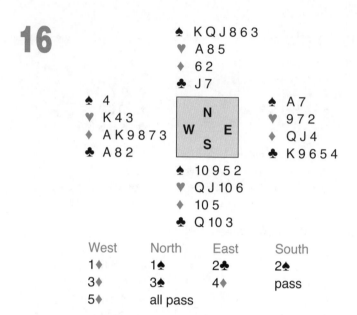

♠ K Q J 8 6 3
♥ A 8 5
♦ 6 2
♣ J 7

♠ 4
♥ K 4 3
♦ A K 9 8 7 3
♣ A 8 2

♠ A 7
♥ 9 7 2
♦ Q J 4
♣ K 9 6 5 4

♠ 10 9 5 2
♥ Q J 10 6
♦ 10 5
♣ Q 10 3

West	North	East	South
1♦	1♠	2♣	2♠
3♦	3♠	4♦	pass
5♦	all pass		

Contract 5♦ by West. North leads ♠K.

Yes, West would like to be in 3NT since, with North on lead, there are nine certain top winners . . . but it's too late for regrets.

As North overcalled 1♠ and 3♠ it is likely that he has ♥A, making South the danger hand. Three heart tricks could be lost if South gained the lead.

Rather than risk South being able to win the third round of clubs (he would return ♥Q), it is better to let North hold his ♠K lead. Even if he switches to another suit, declarer can enter dummy with ♦J and discard a club on ♠A.

Now clubs can be established without losing a trick in the suit by ruffing once, with a top trump, in West's hand. East's ♦Q provides the required entry back to dummy.

17

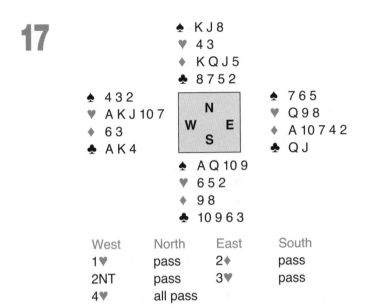

	♠ K J 8		
	♥ 4 3		
	♦ K Q J 5		
	♣ 8 7 5 2		

♠ 4 3 2   ♠ 7 6 5
♥ A K J 10 7   ♥ Q 9 8
♦ 6 3   ♦ A 10 7 4 2
♣ A K 4   ♣ Q J

♠ A Q 10 9
♥ 6 5 2
♦ 9 8
♣ 10 9 6 3

West	North	East	South
1♥	pass	2♦	pass
2NT	pass	3♥	pass
4♥	all pass		

Contract 4♥ by West. North leads ♦K.

There's been some optimistic bidding here and East/West would have paid the price if North had led an initial spade. There would be no way to avoid losing three spades and one diamond. Luckily, North's obvious choice of lead gives declarer an opportunity.

Two things need to be done. Firstly a spade loser in the East hand needs to be discarded. The priority, after winning the first trick, is to play ♣Q, ♣A and ♣K discarding ♠5 from dummy.

This will still leave three small spades in West's hand, which would be losers if trumps were drawn. So, the second thing to be done is to ruff a spade while dummy still has a trump.

West must play two rounds of spades before playing any trumps. This will leave one trump in dummy even if the defence plays trumps every time they get the lead.

Declarer should make ten tricks: one spade ruff in the short hand, five heart tricks, one diamond and three clubs.

18

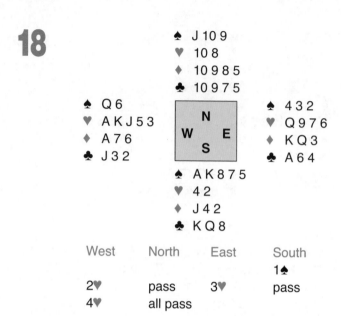

```
              ♠ J 10 9
              ♥ 10 8
              ♦ 10 9 8 5
              ♣ 10 9 7 5
♠ Q 6                        ♠ 4 3 2
♥ A K J 5 3      N           ♥ Q 9 7 6
♦ A 7 6       W     E        ♦ K Q 3
♣ J 3 2          S           ♣ A 6 4
              ♠ A K 8 7 5
              ♥ 4 2
              ♦ J 4 2
              ♣ K Q 8
```

West	North	East	South
			1♠
2♥	pass	3♥	pass
4♥	all pass		

Contract 4♥ by West. North leads ♠J. South cashes ♠A K and plays ♠5.

West should ruff ♠5 with a top heart to guard against the danger of being overruffed with ♥10.

Trumps are drawn in two rounds and declarer's problem is to avoid losing two clubs but counting points should give him the answer. South is known to have just five spades and can be assumed to have both ♣K and ♣Q to give him enough points to open the bidding.

Declarer must play three rounds of diamonds, ending in dummy, and lead a small club towards ♣J 3 2. South is now endplayed. His choice is either to lead a club, allowing both ♣J and ♣A to make, or to give away a ruff and discard.

hands to play

19

♠ A J 10 8 7
♥ A 8
♦ K 10 5
♣ K 5 4

```
      N
   W     E
      S
```

♠ K 9 6
♥ K Q
♦ A J 6 4 3
♣ 7 6 3

West	North	East	South
		1NT	pass
3♠	pass	4♠	all pass

Contract 4♠ by West. North leads ♥J.

20

♠ 7 4 2
♥ K 7 6 4 2
♦ A K 2
♣ A K

```
      N
   W     E
      S
```

♠ A 6 5
♥ A Q 9 3
♦ 9 8 3
♣ 8 7 6

West	North	East	South
1♥	pass	3♥	pass
4♥	all pass		

Contract 4♥ by West. North leads ♠K.

21

♠ A K 2
♥ A 3
♦ A 10 2
♣ A 8 6 5 2

```
      N
   W     E
      S
```

♠ Q 4 3
♥ 10 6
♦ K J 4
♣ K 9 7 4 3

West	North	East	South
1♣	3♥	4♣	pass
6♣	all pass		

Contract 6♣ by West. North leads ♥K.

19

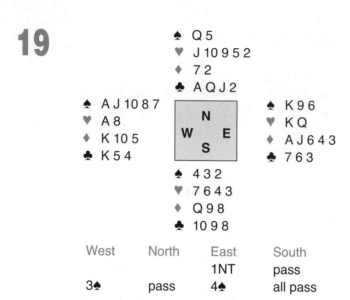

	♠ Q 5	
	♥ J 10 9 5 2	
	♦ 7 2	
	♣ A Q J 2	
♠ A J 10 8 7		♠ K 9 6
♥ A 8		♥ K Q
♦ K 10 5		♦ A J 6 4 3
♣ K 5 4		♣ 7 6 3
	♠ 4 3 2	
	♥ 7 6 4 3	
	♦ Q 9 8	
	♣ 10 9 8	

West	North	East	South
		1NT	pass
3♠	pass	4♠	all pass

Contract 4♠ by West. North leads ♥J.

West should win trick one in his own hand since an entry may be needed to East's hand later in the play.

When you look at the hand carefully, you will notice that South is the danger hand, since three tricks could be lost in clubs if South gained the lead. So plan the play to keep South off lead. This means that trumps should be played so that if a trump trick is lost, it is lost to North. Declarer should cross to ♠K and lead ♠9, letting it run if South plays low. Even if South has ♠Q 4 3 2, the lead is in dummy to repeat the finesse.

On the actual deal North will win and play another heart, won in dummy.

Diamonds too need to be established without letting South get on lead, so ♦3 is played and, when South follows with ♦8, West plays ♦10, again allowing the safe hand to be on lead if the finesse loses.

Even if both the finesses are wrong, the defence can take only ♠Q, ♦Q and ♣A.

20

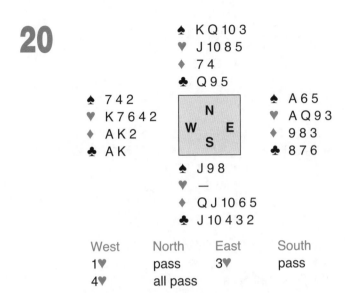

	♠ K Q 10 3	
	♥ J 10 8 5	
	♦ 7 4	
	♣ Q 9 5	

♠ 7 4 2
♥ K 7 6 4 2
♦ A K 2
♣ A K

♠ A 6 5
♥ A Q 9 3
♦ 9 8 3
♣ 8 7 6

♠ J 9 8
♥ —
♦ Q J 10 6 5
♣ J 10 4 3 2

West	North	East	South
1♥	pass	3♥	pass
4♥	all pass		

Contract 4♥ by West. North leads ♠K.

When dummy is exposed the contract looks very secure but that is always the time to look for hidden dangers.

The only problem that can prevent declarer from taking ten tricks is a 4-0 trump break. Nothing can be done to avoid a heart loser if South has four but it is possible to pick up four trumps in the North hand.

To cope with this possibility, declarer must play a small heart to ♥K at trick two. The bad break is revealed but a small trump from West forces North to put up ♥J or ♥10 – otherwise West can finesse ♥9. Now dummy has a finesse position over North. The West hand is re-entered with a club to play another heart.

If ♥A or ♥Q is played from dummy at trick two, it would be too late to recover.

21

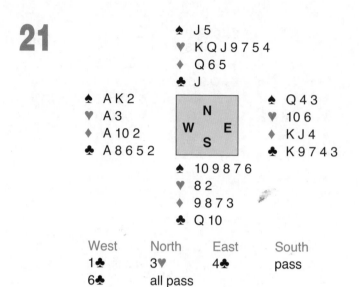

♠ J 5
♥ K Q J 9 7 5 4
♦ Q 6 5
♣ J

♠ A K 2
♥ A 3
♦ A 10 2
♣ A 8 6 5 2

N
W E
S

♠ Q 4 3
♥ 10 6
♦ K J 4
♣ K 9 7 4 3

♠ 10 9 8 7 6
♥ 8 2
♦ 9 8 7 3
♣ Q 10

West	North	East	South
1♣	3♥	4♣	pass
6♣	all pass		

Contract 6♣ by West. North leads ♥K.

A heart must be lost and, therefore, a diamond loser must be avoided. Declarer does not want to risk having to guess who holds ♦Q.

If trumps break 2-1 the contract is certain. ♥A is won, trumps are drawn, ♠A K Q are cashed and declarer lets the defence win its inevitable heart trick. Here, it will be North who wins but it would be exactly the same were it to be South.

Whichever defender wins he must solve the problem of the finesse by leading a diamond or giving away a ruff and discard by playing a spade or a heart.

hands to play

22

♠ A K Q 9 6 4		♠ J 8 7 2
♥ 3 2	N	♥ K J 7 6 5
♦ K 9 5	W E	♦ A 7 3
♣ J 6	S	♣ 7

West	North	East	South
	pass	pass	1♣
2♠	pass	4♠	all pass

Contract 4♠ by West. North leads ♣2. South wins ♣A and returns ♦Q.

23

♠ 3		♠ A Q J 8
♥ A K Q 9 7 5 3	N	♥ J 10 4
♦ 6 3	W E	♦ A 9 4
♣ A 8 3	S	♣ K 9 2

West	North	East	South
1♥	pass	1♠	pass
3♥	pass	6♥	all pass

Contract 6♥ by West. North leads ♦K.

24

♠ A 5 4 3 2		♠ K 8 7
♥ K	N	♥ J 10 9
♦ Q 9 4 2	W E	♦ K J 10 3
♣ K 10 4	S	♣ A 5 3

West	North	East	South
		1NT	pass
3♠	pass	4♠	all pass

Contract 4♠ by West. North leads ♠Q.

22

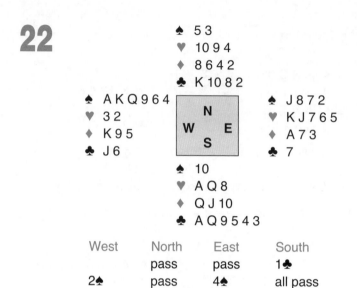

```
                    ♠  5 3
                    ♥  10 9 4
                    ♦  8 6 4 2
                    ♣  K 10 8 2
  ♠ A K Q 9 6 4                        ♠  J 8 7 2
  ♥ 3 2              N                 ♥  K J 7 6 5
  ♦ K 9 5         W     E              ♦  A 7 3
  ♣ J 6              S                 ♣  7
                    ♠  10
                    ♥  A Q 8
                    ♦  Q J 10
                    ♣  A Q 9 5 4 3
```

West	North	East	South
	pass	pass	1♣
2♠	pass	4♠	all pass

Contract 4♠ by West. North leads ♣2. South wins ♣A and returns
♦Q.

There are eight top winners and a ninth trick is easily available by
trumping a club. Hearts will have to produce the tenth trick.

South, after his opening bid, must surely hold ♥A and, if declarer
had to play the suit himself, it would be right to lead a heart
towards dummy and play ♥J. However, South could have both
♥A and ♥Q or, possibly, just ♥Q.

There is an extra chance, which does not cost. After winning the
second trick, drawing trumps and ruffing a club, we have this:

```
  ♠ Q 9 6 4                  ♠  J
  ♥ 3 2           N          ♥  K J 7 6 5
  ♦ K 9        W     E       ♦  7 3
  ♣ —             S          ♣  —
```

West plays ♦K and ♦9. If South has to win this diamond trick, he
will have to give the tenth trick either by leading a heart or by
giving a ruff and discard. Should North win that ♦9, he will have to
lead a heart and declarer must try ♥J as suggested above.

23

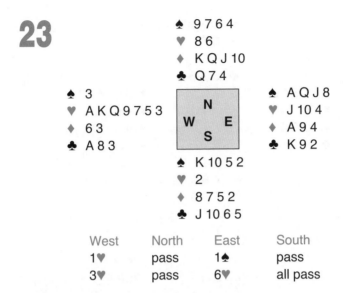

♠ 9 7 6 4
♥ 8 6
♦ K Q J 10
♣ Q 7 4

♠ 3
♥ A K Q 9 7 5 3
♦ 6 3
♣ A 8 3

♠ A Q J 8
♥ J 10 4
♦ A 9 4
♣ K 9 2

♠ K 10 5 2
♥ 2
♦ 8 7 5 2
♣ J 10 6 5

West	North	East	South
1♥	pass	1♠	pass
3♥	pass	6♥	all pass

Contract 6♥ by West. North leads ♦K.

West can count seven heart tricks, one spade, one diamond and two clubs. The twelfth trick will have to come from spades. West wins ♦A and draws trumps.

There are two ways to play for the extra spade trick but only one is 100% certain to make the contract. One is to lead a small spade from the West hand and play dummy's ♠Q if North plays low. If the queen wins, that is the extra trick. However, if it loses, South will play a diamond and that means one down.

The second way to play spades is to take a ruffing finesse. Play to ♠A and lead ♠Q. If South plays ♠K, ruff and return to dummy with a club to discard the losing diamond on ♠J.

But if South does not play ♠K, West discards his diamond. North is welcome to win the spade but the defence now have no diamond trick to cash. When the lead is regained, West can throw the losing club on ♠J.

24

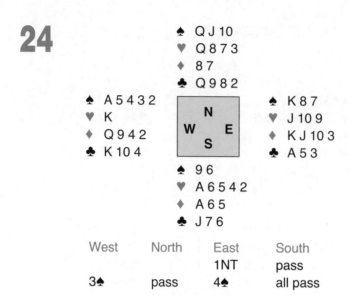

♠ Q J 10
♥ Q 8 7 3
♦ 8 7
♣ Q 9 8 2

♠ A 5 4 3 2
♥ K
♦ Q 9 4 2
♣ K 10 4

♠ K 8 7
♥ J 10 9
♦ K J 10 3
♣ A 5 3

♠ 9 6
♥ A 6 5 4 2
♦ A 6 5
♣ J 7 6

West	North	East	South
		1NT	pass
3♠	pass	4♠	all pass

Contract 4♠ by West. North leads ♠Q.

There is one loser in every suit but it may be possible to discard a club on an established heart in East's hand. Suppose South holds ♥Q. After ♥K has lost to ♥A, East's ♥J 10 offers the opportunity for a ruffing finesse.

There's a small extra chance which is worth a try. Say ♠K wins the first trick and ♥J is led. Maybe South has ♥A, but not ♥Q, and thinks declarer intends to take a heart finesse and let ♥J run. This *could* be the position:

♥ K x  ♥ J 10 9

Unaware of West's distribution, South may not realise the need to rise with ♥A. If so, declarer will steal the vital extra trick. If it is North who has ♥A, there is still time and sufficient entries to try the ruffing finesse. If North switches to a club, care is needed. West wins ♣K, cashes ♠A and plays ♦2 to ♦10 to make sure dummy can be entered twice – once with a diamond, now or later, and with ♣A. On the actual hand 4♠ should fail. However, if there is a chance that a defender might go wrong, it is best to give him the opportunity sooner rather than later.

hands to play

25

♠ A 7 3		♠ K J 2
♥ K 10		♥ 6 5 4
♦ K 4	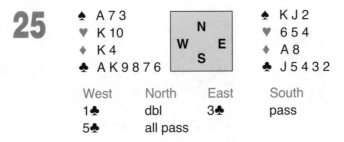	♦ A 8
♣ A K 9 8 7 6		♣ J 5 4 3 2

West	North	East	South
1♣	dbl	3♣	pass
5♣	all pass		

Contract 5♣ by West. North leads ♦Q.

26

♠ J 5 3		♠ Q 8 4 2
♥ A K Q J 10		♥ 9 8 4 3
♦ 5 2	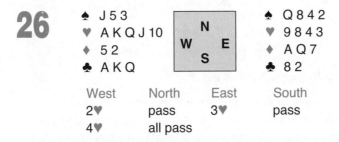	♦ A Q 7
♣ A K Q		♣ 8 2

West	North	East	South
2♥	pass	3♥	pass
4♥	all pass		

Contract 4♥ by West. North leads ♦J.

27

♠ A K 8 5		♠ 7 6 4
♥ A Q J 8 3		♥ K 10 9
♦ 9 5 4	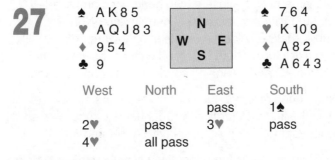	♦ A 8 2
♣ 9		♣ A 6 4 3

West	North	East	South
		pass	1♠
2♥	pass	3♥	pass
4♥	all pass		

Contract 4♥ by West. North leads ♠2.

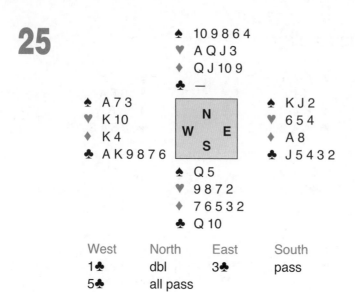

25

	♠ 10 9 8 6 4	
	♥ A Q J 3	
	♦ Q J 10 9	
	♣ —	
♠ A 7 3	**N**	♠ K J 2
♥ K 10	**W E**	♥ 6 5 4
♦ K 4	**S**	♦ A 8
♣ A K 9 8 7 6		♣ J 5 4 3 2
	♠ Q 5	
	♥ 9 8 7 2	
	♦ 7 6 5 3 2	
	♣ Q 10	

West	North	East	South
1♣	dbl	3♣	pass
5♣	all pass		

Contract 5♣ by West. North leads ♦Q.

3NT, preferably with West as declarer, would be an easier contract. West's red suit kings are best protected from a lead through them, though on the actual deal 3NT makes from either side.

Declarer has three possible losers (two hearts and one spade) and only ten sure winners. It is almost certain, after North's takeout double, that he holds ♥A and leading towards ♥K 10 will not make the extra trick. There is a good chance, however, that North also holds ♠Q and a winning spade finesse can be taken.

In fact, if North does hold ♠Q, the contract is secure anyway. Declarer wins the first trick, draws two rounds of trumps, cashes the second top diamond and simply plays ♠A, ♠K and ♠J.

Should North win ♠Q, he is forced to give away the eleventh trick. A heart allows West's ♥K to make and either a spade or a diamond allows declarer to ruff in dummy and throw a losing heart from his own hand.

Here West's reward is to find that South holds ♠Q doubleton.

26

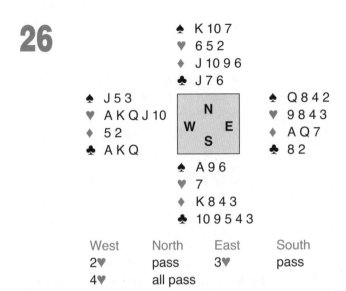

♠ K 10 7
♥ 6 5 2
♦ J 10 9 6
♣ J 7 6

♠ J 5 3
♥ A K Q J 10
♦ 5 2
♣ A K Q

♠ Q 8 4 2
♥ 9 8 4 3
♦ A Q 7
♣ 8 2

♠ A 9 6
♥ 7
♦ K 8 4 3
♣ 10 9 5 4 3

West	North	East	South
2♥	pass	3♥	pass
4♥	all pass		

Contract 4♥ by West. North leads ♦J.

The opening lead makes it likely that South holds ♦K since North would be reluctant to lead ♦J from a holding headed by ♦K J. A diamond finesse will surely lose.

Declarer cannot play spades himself since the probability is that he would have to lose three tricks in the suit to go with the diamond loser. He can, however, arrange for the defenders either to open up the spade suit or let him discard a losing spade.

He should rise with dummy's ♦A, draw trumps and play ♣A K Q, discarding ♦7 from dummy. Declarer now plays a diamond, giving the player who wins the trick a choice of losing alternatives. A diamond allows declarer to trump in dummy and discard a spade from his hand and a spade establishes a winner for him.

27

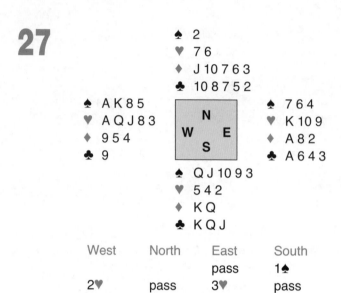

```
                    ♠ 2
                    ♥ 7 6
                    ♦ J 10 7 6 3
                    ♣ 10 8 7 5 2
♠ A K 8 5          N              ♠ 7 6 4
♥ A Q J 8 3     W     E           ♥ K 10 9
♦ 9 5 4            S              ♦ A 8 2
♣ 9                               ♣ A 6 4 3
                    ♠ Q J 10 9 3
                    ♥ 5 4 2
                    ♦ K Q
                    ♣ K Q J
```

West	North	East	South
		pass	1♠
2♥	pass	3♥	pass
4♥	all pass		

Contract 4♥ by West. North leads ♠2.

With North leading partner's suit, ♠2 is surely a singleton. If West wins ♠A and draws trumps there are only nine winners and he will lose two spades and two diamonds. Trying to ruff a spade in dummy won't work either because North will trump ♠K and declarer will still be a trick short.

However, with the equivalent of top trumps in dummy, West can get home by ruffing three clubs in his own hand and using dummy's trumps to draw the opponents trumps – a dummy reversal.

West should win ♠A and play a club to ♣A, ruff a club with ♥A – it always looks spectacular, a diamond to ♦A, ruff another club high, a trump to dummy and ruff the last club. Now play a trump to dummy and draw the last trump. West still has ♠K for the tenth trick.

Note that it is better to cross to dummy with the non trump entries first, just in case South could discard a diamond on the fourth club and then trump ♦A.

hands to play

28

♠ A 4 3 2	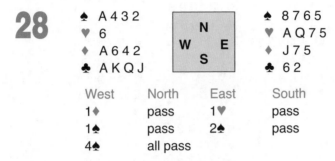	♠ 8 7 6 5
♥ 6		♥ A Q 7 5
♦ A 6 4 2		♦ J 7 5
♣ A K Q J		♣ 6 2

West	North	East	South
1♦	pass	1♥	pass
1♠	pass	2♠	pass
4♠	all pass		

Contract 4♠ by West. North leads ♣10.

29

♠ A J 10 5	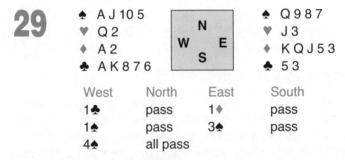	♠ Q 9 8 7
♥ Q 2		♥ J 3
♦ A 2		♦ K Q J 5 3
♣ A K 8 7 6		♣ 5 3

West	North	East	South
1♣	pass	1♦	pass
1♠	pass	3♠	pass
4♠	all pass		

Contract 4♠ by West. North leads ♦10, which you win with ♦A.
You lay down ♠A and North throws a heart.

30

♠ Q 9	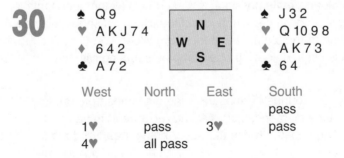	♠ J 3 2
♥ A K J 7 4		♥ Q 10 9 8
♦ 6 4 2		♦ A K 7 3
♣ A 7 2		♣ 6 4

West	North	East	South
			pass
1♥	pass	3♥	pass
4♥	all pass		

Contract 4♥ by West. North leads ♣10.

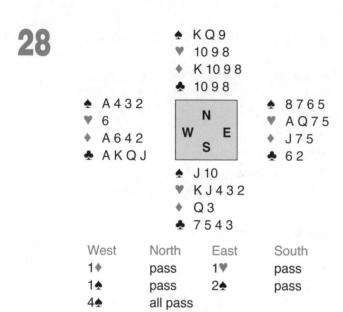

```
                    ♠ K Q 9
                    ♥ 10 9 8
                    ♦ K 10 9 8
                    ♣ 10 9 8
♠ A 4 3 2                          ♠ 8 7 6 5
♥ 6              N                 ♥ A Q 7 5
♦ A 6 4 2    W       E             ♦ J 7 5
♣ A K Q J        S                 ♣ 6 2
                    ♠ J 10
                    ♥ K J 4 3 2
                    ♦ Q 3
                    ♣ 7 5 4 3
```

West	North	East	South
1♦	pass	1♥	pass
1♠	pass	2♠	pass
4♠	all pass		

Contract 4♠ by West. North leads ♣10.

North probably leads a club, as it is the unbid suit. West can see two spade and three diamond losers. There are eight winners and discarding the diamonds on the clubs will allow the ruffing of a diamond in dummy, but a bit more ruffing may be needed to bring the total to ten tricks.

The problem is that the trump pips are so poor that an overruff by the defenders is quite possible. If West draws all the opponents' trumps there won't be enough for ruffing, So West should play a small trump from both hands at trick two. When West regains the lead, ♠A is cashed, leaving one trump outstanding with the enemy.

Now play four rounds of clubs throwing diamonds from dummy. Play ♦A, ruff a diamond, cash ♥A and ruff a heart in hand. Another diamond and ruff in dummy. Another heart and ruff in hand. At any stage North can ruff in with his trump but you will only lose two spades and one diamond. Try it and see.

29

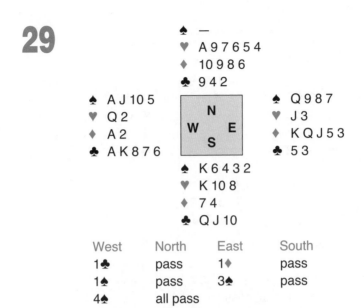

	♠ —	
	♥ A 9 7 6 5 4	
	♦ 10 9 8 6	
	♣ 9 4 2	
♠ A J 10 5		♠ Q 9 8 7
♥ Q 2		♥ J 3
♦ A 2		♦ K Q J 5 3
♣ A K 8 7 6		♣ 5 3
	♠ K 6 4 3 2	
	♥ K 10 8	
	♦ 7 4	
	♣ Q J 10	

West	North	East	South
1♣	pass	1♦	pass
1♠	pass	3♠	pass
4♠	all pass		

Contract 4♠ by West. North leads ♦10, which you win with ♦A. You lay down ♠A and North throws a heart.

You feel pretty confident when dummy goes down. This is a good contract and defenders have not found the best lead. Surely you can only lose two hearts and a trump.

You win ♦A and play ♠A – North shows out. Don't panic, these things happen occasionally! But you must stop playing trumps as South has too many for you to draw.

Cash ♣A K and ruff a club in dummy. Play ♦K Q. South ruffs ♦Q but you overruff and play another club ruffing in dummy.

South can overruff that club with his king, cash two heart winners and play a trump. But you win in dummy and play another winning diamond. South ruffs, you overruff and draw South's last trump and cash your club winner.

Play the cards through to see how you can make South's spades disappear by forcing him to ruff. Of course if South does not ruff the diamonds you can throw your losing hearts away.

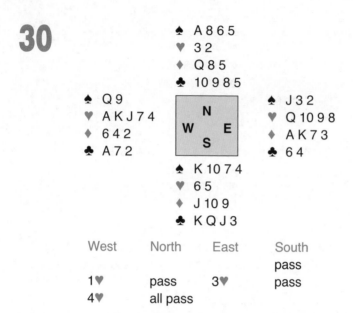

30

```
            ♠  A 8 6 5
            ♥  3 2
            ♦  Q 8 5
            ♣  10 9 8 5
♠  Q 9                          ♠  J 3 2
♥  A K J 7 4        N           ♥  Q 10 9 8
♦  6 4 2       W       E        ♦  A K 7 3
♣  A 7 2           S            ♣  6 4
            ♠  K 10 7 4
            ♥  6 5
            ♦  J 10 9
            ♣  K Q J 3
```

West	North	East	South
			pass
1♥	pass	3♥	pass
4♥	all pass		

Contract 4♥ by West. North leads ♣10.

There are four potential losers: two spades, one diamond and one club.

There is no chance of discarding the club loser but it might be possible to establish a spade winner in time to discard a diamond from West's hand.

The opening lead sometimes provides valuable inferences. Here it looks probable that South can be placed with ♣K Q J. Since South did not open the bidding, he will not hold both ♠A K as well. If North holds both ♠A K, he might have preferred to lead a top spade. So it is likely that ♠A and ♠K are in different hands and the best chance is to play South for ♠10. The 50% chance that South holds ♠10 is a better bet.

West should win ♣A, draw trumps and play ♠2 towards ♠Q 9. When South plays low, West tries ♠9 and North has to win with ♠A. Declarer regains the lead in time to knock out ♠K and establish a spade trick for a diamond discard. One spade, five hearts, two diamonds, ♣A and a club ruff make up the required ten tricks.

Really Easy Bridge

Really Easy Bridge
http://www.reallyeasybridge.com/
is the special website of the English Bridge Union
dedicated to all things Really Easy.

- It provides details of the up and coming
events run by the EBU for Novice and Improver
players, together with results of
previous events.

- Details of the books in the Really Easy series

- Tips and hints on bidding

- Comprehensive list of bridge terms

English Bridge Union
Broadfields, Bicester Road,
Aylesbury HP19 8AZ
Tel: 01296 317200
Fax: 01296 317220
Email: postmaster@ebu.co.uk

index of key words